Lucky Stars

Lori Reid is an astrologer, one of the UK's top hand analysts and a prolific writer of bestselling books for adults and children on dreams and related subjects. As an expert in her field she is regularly featured on radio and television in the UK, and her weekly astrological column is syndicated in both national and international newspapers. Currently Lori writes the astrological forecast page for *Best* magazine and is a daily contributor to the *Daily Mail*'s 'Femail' website.

Lucky Stars

A teenager's guide to fame and fortune

Lori Reid

RIDER

LONDON • SYDNEY • AUCKLAND • JOHANNESBURG

3 5 7 9 10 8 6 4 2

First published in 2002 by Rider
an imprint of Ebury Press, Random House
20 Vauxhall Bridge Road, London SW1V 2SA

Random House Australia (Pty) Limited
20 Alfred Street, Milsons Point, Sydney
New South Wales 2061, Australia

Random House New Zealand Limited
18 Poland Road, Glenfield
Auckland 10, New Zealand

Random House South Africa (Pty) Limited
Endulini, 5A Jubilee Road
Parktown 2193, South Africa

The Random House Group Limited Reg. No. 954009

Papers used by Rider are natural, recyclable products made from wood
grown in sustainable forests.

Printed and bound by Mackays of Chatham plc, Chatham, Kent

Illustrations by Rob Loxston

A CIP catalogue record for this book
is available from the British Library

ISBN 0-7126-5738-X

Contents

Lucky You!

Welcome to *Lucky Stars* – the book that reveals why you're so special. Whether you're a Gemini, a Leo, a Pisces or whatever, your astrological sign will show you why you're lucky to be you. Read about your sign and you'll discover a whole lot more about yourself, too – such as your true character and what makes you tick, your likes and dislikes, your talents and how they can bring you good fortune in life. You'll also find out how to recognise the flaws in your character and learn how to overcome them by accentuating the positive. And, of course, *love*. Your deepest feelings, your hopes and wishes, what you're like in a relationship – all will be revealed, as well as whom you get on with best, who your soul-link is and who simply drives you up the wall!

But *Lucky Stars* takes you further than most other books on sun-sign astrology because it enables you to work out your *rising sign*. While your birth, or sun, sign represents your fundamental character and personality, your rising sign shows how you behave in the outside world – how you look, how you like to dress, how others see you and how you come across when people first meet you. Together, the characteristics indicated by your sun and rising sign make you the unique and very special individual that you are.

Your sun and rising signs are your mirrors of fortune. Read up on them and bask in your own wonderful reflection.

The Signs of the Zodiac

ARIES – The Ram

21 March – 20 April

- Planetary ruler: Mars

- Key characteristics: energetic, pioneering, impulsive, creative, enthusiastic, restless. Natural leader. Seeks the way ahead.

TAURUS – The Bull

21 April – 21 May

- Planetary ruler: Venus

- Key characteristics: practical, down to earth, strong willed. Lover of beauty and nature. Seeks emotional and material security.

GEMINI – The Twins

22 May – 22 June

- Planetary ruler: Mercury

- Key characteristics: restless, curious, alert, versatile. Master juggler. Brilliant communicator. Seeker of knowledge and inspiration.

CANCER – The Crab

23 June – 23 July

- Planetary ruler: the moon

- Key characteristics: emotional, intuitive and nostalgic. Has tough outer shell, but is soft and sensitive inside. Family-oriented and lover of Nature. Seeks to maintain links.

LEO – The Lion

24 July – 23 August

- Planetary ruler: the sun

- Key characteristics: charismatic, enthusiastic, courageous, loyal, kind. Dramatic. Needs to be centre-stage and in charge. Seeks creative expression.

VIRGO – The Maiden

24 August – 23 September

- Planetary ruler: Mercury

- Key characteristics: adaptable, critical, helpful, sympathetic. Animal lover. Appreciates attention to detail. Seeks and strives for perfection.

LIBRA – The Scales

24 September – 23 October

- Planetary ruler: Venus

- Key characteristics: thoughtful, sensitive, charming, diplomatic. Loves beauty, balance and luxury. Upholder of justice. Seeks harmony in everything.

SCORPIO – The Scorpion

24 October – 22 November

- Planetary rulers: Pluto and Mars

- Key characteristics: loyal, committed, never forgets a slight. Has deep inner feelings and penetrating insight. Intuitive healer. Seeks the elusive, the mysterious and the unknown.

SAGITTARIUS – The Archer

23 November – 21 December

- Planetary ruler: Jupiter

- Key characteristics: optimistic, enthusiastic, generous, funny. Adventurous risk-taker. Lover of travel and philosophy. Seeks the opportunity to take light into dark places.

CAPRICORN – The Goat

22 December – 20 January

- Planetary ruler: Saturn

- Key characteristics: ambitious, practical, disciplined, resourceful, organised. Achievement-driven. Wry sense of humour. Seeks status, position and power.

AQUARIUS – The Water Carrier

21 January – 19 February

- Planetary rulers: Uranus and Saturn

- Key characteristics: loyal, idealistic, independent, unconventional. Far-sighted. Hates restriction and limitation. Seeks reform for the greater good.

PISCES – The Fishes

20 February – 20 March

- Planetary rulers: Neptune and Jupiter

- Key characteristics: sensitive, caring, intuitive, imaginative, poetic. Creative dreamer. Romantic and vulnerable. Seeks Nirvana.

Lucky Stars

The influence of the planets

Each planet is associated with a specific set of qualities. Knowing a little about the individual nature of the planets will give you a greater understanding of how they affect us in general – and your sign in particular. Incidentally, although technically the sun is a star and the moon is a satellite, astrologically and for the sake of simplicity, they are referred to as planets.

The *sun* represents your individuality – your innermost essence which expresses your creativity, your vitality, your goals, your will and your determination. It is your masculine side. The sun is the planetary ruler of everyone born under the sign of Leo.

The *moon* represents your feelings, emotions, sensitivities and imagination. It throws light on the subconscious and unconscious mind and is your feminine side. The moon is the planetary ruler of everyone born under the sign of Cancer.

Mercury, the planet of communication, shows how you think and express yourself. It represents your mental ability, your cleverness and astuteness. Mercury governs two signs and is the planetary ruler of everyone born under Gemini and Virgo.

Venus shows how you relate to other people both socially and in loving and romantic situations. It represents your artistic talents and, as the 'Lesser Fortune' of the zodiac, it also reveals where your luck lies. Like Mercury, Venus governs two signs and is the planetary ruler of everyone born under Taurus and Libra.

Mars symbolises physical energy and represents your stamina, initiative and sexual drive. It shows how you stand up for yourself and reveals your fighting spirit. Mars is the planetary ruler of everyone born under the sign of Aries and also shares rulership with Pluto for the sign of Scorpio.

Jupiter shows where your opportunities lie and reveals your ability to expand your knowledge and understanding. It also indicates how you like to enjoy yourself. As the 'Greater Fortune' of the zodiac , it represents your lucky side and potential for wealth. Jupiter is the planetary ruler of everyone born under the sign of Sagittarius and also shares rulership with Neptune for the sign of Pisces.

Saturn represents your self-discipline, strength of character and sense of responsibility. It's linked with hard work, tenacity and persistence and is often considered the hard task-master of the zodiac. Saturn is the planetary ruler of everyone born under the sign of Capricorn and also shares rulership with Uranus for the sign of Aquarius.

Uranus shows the ways in which you reveal your originality, creativity and powers of invention. It is known as the visionary planet since it is concerned with the ability to see into the

future, inspiring revolutionary ideas and breaking new ground. Uranus is the planetary ruler of Aquarius.

Neptune reflects your sensitivity and your attraction to idealism and mysticism. It is concerned with escape from everyday problems through imagination, illusion and dreams – without which we wouldn't be able to see the greater picture. Neptune is the planetary ruler of everyone born under the sign of Pisces.

Pluto shows how you can develop, regenerate and transform yourself and your environment. It is concerned with deep, hidden feelings and emotional beliefs and attitudes. Pluto is the planetary ruler of everyone born under the sign of Scorpio.

In your element

Each sign of the zodiac belongs to one of four elements – Fire, Earth, Air and Water. The element group your sign belongs to is associated with certain characteristics. For example, belonging to the element Fire means you are probably fiery and volatile by nature, whereas if you belong to the Water element you tend to be more fluid and changeable.

Each of the four groups contains three signs. Find your sign and discover how your ruling element influences you and the way you do things.

Group: Fire

Signs: Aries, Leo, Sagittarius
Element influence: energetic, dynamic, enthusiastic, friendly, open, impetuous

- Aries Fire is red, hot and smouldering

- Leo Fire is glowing gold, warm and illuminating

- Sagittarius Fire is flashing blue with inspiration

Group: Earth

Signs: Taurus, Virgo, Capricorn
Element influence: practical, choosy, emotionally stable, cautious, full of common sense

- Taurus Earth is warm, supportive and comfortable

- Virgo Earth holds the practical secrets of survival

- Capricorn Earth provides a solid foundation

Group: Air

Signs: Gemini, Libra, Aquarius
Element influence: sociable, chatty, idealistic, logical, restless, full of ideas

- Gemini Air seeks the buzz and to spread the knowledge

- Libra Air tunes in to harmony to find balance

- Aquarius Air looks ahead to ideas of the future

Group: Water

Signs: Cancer, Scorpio, Pisces
Element influence: caring, emotional, impressionable, changeable, intuitive, responsive

- Cancer Water bubbles, flows and surrounds

- Scorpio Water freezes and holds memory

- Pisces Water is misty-moist and mysterious

People born under signs belonging to the same element have something special in common because they tend to operate on the same level and experience life in a similar kind of way. This means that you're likely to be most in tune with natives of your own element. Understanding the dynamics of the elements and how they interact can also give you insights into relationships. Find out where your affinities lie in the chart below.

Lucky Stars

	Water	Air	Earth	Fire
Fire	Fire finds Water emotionally demanding, while Water finds Fire challenging and overpowering.	Because you provide each other with interesting and stimulating ideas, you are highly compatible.	Fire finds Earth dull and slow, while Earth finds Fire pushy and too flamboyant.	Fire signs understand each other well, although sometimes they have a problem with who should be boss.
Earth	You support each other well and together you can flourish. You are well suited and compatible.	Earth finds Air impractical and too airy-fairy, while Air feels pressurised and constricted by Earth.	You understand each other well, but you must avoid getting bogged down and becoming bored with each other.	
Air	Air finds Water overpowering, while Water is uncomfortable with Air because Water never quite knows what Air will do next.	You two understand each other because you can communicate quickly and with ease. You're on the same wavelength.		
Water	You understand each other's feelings deeply, and can have the most rewarding relationship. Take care, though, not to cut yourselves off from everyone else.			

The Sun Signs

Lucky Stars

Aries ♈
The Ram

21 March – 20 April
Ruling planet: Mars
Element: Fire

Why you're lucky to be you!

Well, principally because you're *first* – where you go, others follow. It's your place in the zodiac – in pole position and leading the rest of the signs – that gives you a sense of importance and responsibility. You're daring and adventurous and you simply love taking action. What's more, you're lucky to have strong physical and mental energy, coupled with a great sense of humour which helps you and those around you through difficult times. Other people admire you for your fearlessness and zest. You aim to win, and as long as you stay focused you're able to attract lots of good fortune.

You're a star because:

You have such a dynamic personality. You're a born leader, direct but friendly, with an indomitable spirit and an irrepressible nature. And, of course, you love a challenge. Perhaps that's

because you have a need to prove something to yourself – as well as to others! It's not enough for you to talk about things – you want to go out there and get some action going. And when it comes to sport, you're simply fearless. If anyone was ever born to be a champion, it was you.

Your special qualities

You start projects with lots of good, creative ideas and you have the knack of being able to fire others with enthusiasm and get them motivated. If there's anything new starting, you're there at the front of the pack, and when you have a goal in mind there's absolutely no stopping you. Defeat simply isn't in your vocabulary. If things aren't going your way, you're out of the door fast with a new idea already forming in your mind. You like fame – not necessarily the fortune – but you do want to be recognised for what you do rather than for what you've got in the bank. You're the competitor of the zodiac and without you lots of things just wouldn't ever happen.

However...

Note the number of unfinished projects you have sitting around on shelves or scattered about in your room! When the novelty has worn off, you just lose interest, don't you? So whilst you're a great starter, you have to admit you're a bit of a poor finisher. Patience truly is a virtue, but where you're concerned it's in very short supply. The truth is, you're impulsive; you don't like taking advice from others and all too often your rash actions can land you right in it. And, let's be honest, there are very few Aries who weren't born with a sizeable dollop of the selfish rascal in their nature!

The balancing act

Learning by experience really does bring wisdom. Notice how using force or aggression to get your own way makes you unpopular and results in others responding aggressively. It brings you nothing but a heap of grief. Try not to jump into the deep end so impulsively; instead, give yourself more time to think before you act. Be prepared to use tact, diplomacy and discussion. Learn to delegate to others the things you know they can develop better than you can. Everyone has his or her own particular skills – recognise that and give credit to others where and when it's due. If you're not sure about something, be prepared to ask for advice. Let your motto be, *'look and listen before you leap'*.

The mirror effect

There's a hidden factor which many people overlook when they read about their sun sign – the *mirror effect*. Essentially, this is all about understanding your opposite sign. You see, your opposite sign is your shadow self – your other half. It complements and provides the missing links to your own character and nature. As an Aries, your opposite sign is Libra. Understanding and adopting some of the characteristics associated with people born under that sign will help you not only to become a much more rounded person, but also to attract more good fortune into your own life. For example, Libra can show you how to:

- get what you want *subtly* so as not to make enemies

- gain deeper insights into love and romance

- improve your health, looks and style

But there's so much more that you can learn from Libra, and throughout life you'll find that this sign holds the answers to many of the dilemmas and problems which you as an Aries will experience. Aries and Libra are but two sides of the same coin, and together they make a formidable team. So, find out more by turning to your opposite sign and taking a leaf out of Libra's book.

Your love nature

With the planet Mars as your ruler you're just plain sexy! Mars also makes you dynamic – and whether you're female or male, you do like to do the chasing. You're deeply romantic, too, and you're particularly skilled in the charming chat-up routine when moving in for the kill. You love nothing better than the thrill of the chase and, of course, making a conquest, so you're likely to have quite a few exciting, short-term liaisons. However, once

you really fall in love, you make a good partner who can keep things going in fresh and exciting ways. There's a tendency for Aries to dominate a partnership and this is where your opposite sign Libra can give you some tips for adopting a more sharing role. And some Aries are so sporty, active and busy that they can run/jog past their greatest love without even realising it. So, slow down, Aries; you don't want to be in such a rush that you miss out!

Lucky Stars

Cosmic combinations

Whom do you get on with best? Who sets your heart on fire, puts a smile on your lips and colour in your cheeks? Who brings you bliss and who gives you misery? Do you drive each other wild or up the wall? Check your love chart to find out.

Aries	going places together	♥♥♥♥
Taurus	dull	♥♥
Gemini	fun and games	♥♥♥♥
Cancer	too clingy and emotional	♥♥
Leo	passionate!	♥♥♥♥♥
Virgo	far too slow	♥
Libra	attraction of opposites	♥♥♥♥
Scorpio	sexy challenge!	♥♥♥♥
Sagittarius	fiery adventure	♥♥♥♥♥
Capricorn	let it grow	♥♥♥
Aquarius	good times	♥♥♥♥
Pisces	dream on	♥♥

♥ = no-no	♥♥♥♥ = cool couple
♥♥ = so-so	♥♥♥♥♥ = star match!
♥♥♥ = hang in there	

Talents and interests

Your sign corresponds to speed and action and it brings out in you a natural talent for sport. It gives you a competitive edge and a need to win. So, whether on a tennis court or a football pitch, climbing up a mountain or abseiling down a building, you're going to be fearless and completely in your element. You like to keep fit and love to explore different ways to keep

trim. You're adventurous and enjoy travelling. Mars, your ruler, also rules metal instruments, so you're adept at using sharp tools in all kinds of creative pursuits.

Study, work and career paths

Being an Aries means that when you study, especially for exams, your attention tends to be focused in short, sharp bursts. Work out, take some exercise or even play loud music in between intense sessions of concentration to clear your mind and release pent-up energy. Write yourself a timetable giving equal time for work and play – and stick to it, come what may. When writing essays or sitting exams, don't be hasty. Give your subconscious time to work things out. Write a little schema of your answer in the margin before you begin. And when you've finished, read over carefully to correct any mistakes.

You're at your best when you're involved in pioneering work or at the leading edge in whatever career you choose. Scientific and pioneering research, engineering, mechanics or a job involving driving would suit you well. You'd also make a good inventor, designer, firefighter, engine driver, psychiatrist or dentist. Professional sports, too, are a big draw. Whatever you do in life, remember that you hate to be confined, so beware the office job that keeps you in one place all the time.

Health and beauty

Keeping fit is a priority for Aries, so exercise of any kind is a good outlet for your natural energy. You need to fuel your body with top-quality food, veggies and fruit – snacking on junk food is a big no-no. Aries rules the head, so accidents can leave their mark here – and you tend to get headaches when

you're under stress or have a fever. But because you're blessed with a strong constitution and the ability to recover from illness quickly, you're not always patient with yourself or with others who are feeling under the weather.

Female Aries are usually strong and slim, with reddish highlights in thick curly or wavy hair. They often have high cheekbones with an attractive and healthy glow to their complexions. Male Aries tend to have broad foreheads, long noses, prominent eyebrows and an athletic body – a bit like a Greek god! Hair products are high on your beauty-care list and you prefer natural, herbal types of shampoo, make-up and sunscreen when you're climbing those mountains!

Sign Associations

Birthstones: ruby, diamond, bloodstone

Flowers: red rose, gladiolus

Colour: scarlet

Trees: pine, holly, chestnut

Bird: hawk

Animals: sheep (ram), wolf, dragon

Foods: spices, herbs, radish

Countries: England, Denmark, Germany

Body part: the head

Taurus ♉
The Bull

21 April – 21 May
Ruling planet: Venus
Element: Earth

Why you're lucky to be you!

Being born in the second sign of the zodiac and belonging to the element Earth makes you one of life's natural builders and providers. Your strong and practical nature wants to make sure that all is comfortable and secure in your world and that you have plenty of resources to keep everything going. You appreciate beautiful things and you like to have them! You're immensely capable and know how to use your gifts and talents in the most practical of ways. You can always be relied on to produce the cups of tea/coffee for the gang (not forgetting the cream buns!) and you'll organise brilliantly just about anything, from a party to a car boot sale (ensuring you come out in profit, too!). You're solid and sensible and, because you instinctively know what is required in most situations, you tend to attract luck. Above all, you're loved and appreciated by your friends for your reliability and your heart of pure gold.

You're a star because:

You're warm-hearted, can flirt with charm and you're a great cuddler. Your natural eye for beauty and colour means that you excel in the worlds of art, fashion and design, while your rhythmic talents make you an accomplished dancer or musician. When it comes to animals and plant life, you're a natural. You appreciate gardens, trees and landscapes, and are happy rambling about the countryside collecting this and that to take home and arrange creatively. Purposeful and determined, you keep going long after everyone else has flagged. You never give up until you've achieved your goal.

Your special qualities

Your determination, strength of character and ability to work hard give you the edge on other would-be achievers. You seek success and because you're not a quitter: you focus on what you're doing until you get the reward you seek. You're blessed with masses of common sense and a great brain for planning, organising and efficiency. And with that discerning eye of yours, you can spot a good deal a mile off – which comes in handy when you're out shopping or looking for bargains!

However...

You can be a bit of a busybody and a know-it-all. And since your opinions are strong, you tend to be critical of others. You're a great collector, not only of things but also of people! Indeed, you're notorious for hanging on to what you believe you own. And it's this possessive nature that can give rise to a vice that's common amongst Taureans – jealousy! Whilst on the subject of vices, greed is another one that belongs to this sign, for you do have a large appetite – especially a love of sweet

things. Though you're an industrious creature, you like to go at your own pace and hate being pushed or made to feel uncomfortable. You can be a bit of a couch potato and often need a kick-start, which you know is good for you even if you do resent it at first.

The balancing act

When you want your own way, you can come on a bit strong. And because you're stubborn, when you dig in those heels it's virtually impossible to shift you. Such behaviour can get other people's backs up, but by learning the art of persuasion, by quietly and purposefully putting your case across and presenting a logical argument with the right facts and figures, you'll get what you want sooner and go further in life. Be prepared, too, for the odd disappointment when you discover that others don't have quite the same amount of common sense that you do.

The mirror effect

There's a hidden factor which many people overlook when they read about their sun sign – the *mirror effect*. Essentially, this is all about understanding your opposite sign. You see, your opposite sign is your shadow self – your other half. It complements and provides the missing links to your own character and nature. Your opposite sign is Scorpio. Understanding and adopting some of the characteristics associated with people born under this sign will help you not only to become a much

more rounded person, but also to attract more good fortune into your own life. For example, Scorpio can show you how to:

- come across more powerfully and persuasively
- gain deeper insights into the sensual arts of love and romance
- improve your health, personality and performance

But there's so much more that you can learn from Scorpio, and throughout life you'll find that this sign holds the answers to many of the dilemmas and problems which you as a Taurean will experience. Taurus and Scorpio are but two sides of the same coin, and together they make a formidable team. So, find out more by turning to your opposite sign and taking a leaf out of Scorpio's book.

Your love nature

Your planetary ruler is Venus, and since she is the goddess of love she has endowed you with a very loving nature. However, you can be a bit slow off the mark when it comes to romancing, because you're quite choosy. Once you decide someone's right for you, though, you can be very persistent. In fact, when you fall in love, you're totally committed to remain loyal. The senses play a prominent role in the life of all Taureans and you instinctively know how to set the scene for romance – with perfume, low lights, flowers, good food and sensual music. You're sexy in a refined way and love the glamour of the chase.

Cosmic combinations

Whom do you get on with best? Who sets your heart on fire, puts a smile on your lips and colour in your cheeks? Who

brings you bliss and who gives you misery? Do you drive each other wild or up the wall? Check your love chart to find out.

Aries	too fast and fiery	❤❤
Taurus	dead sensual duo	❤❤❤❤
Gemini	get real!	❤
Cancer	sensitively deep	❤❤❤❤
Leo	challenging passion	❤❤❤
Virgo	earthly bliss	❤❤❤❤❤
Libra	tasteful indulgence	❤❤❤
Scorpio	attraction of opposites	❤❤❤❤
Sagittarius	perrr – leeease!	❤
Capricorn	the full works	❤❤❤❤❤
Aquarius	freaky friend	❤❤
Pisces	sensitive heartstrings	❤❤❤

❤ = no-no ❤❤❤❤ = cool couple
❤❤ = so-so ❤❤❤❤❤ = star match!
❤❤❤ = hang in there

Talents and interests

Wherever you live, you need to be in contact with Nature. You're born with green fingers, even if you don't realise it yet! Getting a party together – the friends, the music, the food – is your top talent. You enjoy company and love watching others having fun! Your voice is an asset, and it usually has a distinctive sound. Many Taureans love to sing (sometimes loudly!), and appreciate melody and traditional music. You are in tune with fashion and design, especially the historical aspects of costume and architecture. Your eye for colour is good, and you

particularly appreciate pastel shades. You're a tactile person so you hugely enjoy all forms of craft-work especially if they involve creating with different textures and fabrics.

Study, work and career paths

Routine is important to you, so when you're studying it's best to pace yourself. Don't, whatever you do, leave assignments or revision to the last minute – little and often is your key to success. Keep up to date with your notes and do your homework consistently and in plenty of time. Get a good night's sleep before important tests or exams – remember, you like and need your creature comforts. If you're comfortable in mind and body, you'll perform at your best. And on that subject, never sit an exam on an empty stomach – and make sure you go to the toilet before entering that examination hall.

Your sign suggests an interesting mixture of possible career paths you would enjoy. There's the creative route, taking in the beauty business, arts, crafts and design, architecture, sculpture, jewellery and antiques. You're good with money, too, so may be drawn to the world of finance. The property business, auctioneering, banking, accountancy or the Civil Service would also suit. Alternatively, because you love Nature so much, you would find great satisfaction in horticulture, agriculture or floristry. Whatever route you pursue, you have a strong need for security so are likely to stay in the same job or line of business for a long time.

Health and beauty

In truth, you're a little lazy about keeping fit and by far prefer to *watch* sport than actively participate in it. Taureans, though,

can easily put on extra weight, so if you want to stay healthy and fit without too much hassle, go for the gentler types of exercise such as yoga and t'ai chi. They would suit you right down to the ground. But if you do nothing else, you can at least dance! However, you're very lucky because you have an amazing constitution and can very quickly fight off illness.

There's something very attractive about female Taureans. They usually have masses of curly or wavy hair, and a squarish face with large eyes and lovely lips. Taurus males tend to have a square jaw line and a friendly face, also with attractive eyes. They, too, usually have curly hair, and they appear rather hunky, chunky and cuddly! Taurus rules the throat and the neck, which is sometimes thicker than usual in both sexes. This is a vulnerable area for infections. Aromatherapy oils, sage tea and hot drinks of honey and lemon can help.

Sign Associations

Birthstone: emerald

Flowers: pink rose

Colours: green, light blue, pink

Trees: almond, apple, sycamore

Bird: swan

Animals: bull, elephant

Foods: chocolate, potatoes

Countries: Ireland, Cyprus, Iran

Body parts: throat, neck, ears

Gemini ♊

The Twins

22 May – 22 June
Ruling planet: Mercury
Element: Air

Why you're lucky to be you!

Your job as the third sign of the zodiac and the first belonging to the element of Air is to show others how to communicate. When it comes to writing and literature, you're unsurpassed. No one can touch you where the powers of self-expression are involved. You're witty, you're funny, you're a brilliant mimic and you have everyone in stitches as soon as you open your mouth. Of course, there are those who say you would win an Olympic gold in talking if there was such an event, but since you're so amusing, who cares? You're the best at getting the buzz on the block, seeking out the info and spreading the news. There's a touch of glamour, too, about your role as a news-hound and you're amazing in that you can talk to anyone, from a prince to a pauper. More than anything, you're everybody's friend and nobody's enemy.

You're a star because:

You are lucky enough to have a double nature and this makes you a skilful juggler. You're able, for example, to carry on four conversations at the same time without ever losing the thread, or to do three jobs at the same time – all equally well. It's almost as if you know the secret of cloning and have got it off to a fine art! What's more, you have the gift of the gab and enough charm to talk the birds out of the trees. Your mind is razor-sharp and can conjure ideas out of thin air. You're cheeky, but you're so clever you not only get out of the tightest of scrapes, but emerge with flying colours into the bargain.

Your special qualities

Although some may think you rather frivolous in the way you operate, your greatest strength (thanks to your ruling planet, Mercury) is a mind like quicksilver. Strangely enough, whether it's a mental or physical challenge, you're often there and back before the others have even started. So you're able to absorb much knowledge and many experiences in a short space of time. Throughout your life, you retain a youthful quality which helps you mix with all ages, for you instinctively know how to put people at their ease. You make a wonderful friend, witty and willing to party and play games. And when it comes to word or card games, no one is a patch on you.

However...

Okay, so you're often accused of being a social 'butterfly', flitting from one thing (or person!) to another. It's all because boredom is a prime problem for Gemini, so you do have a tendency to abandon things in midstream. You can also be

forgetful, which can land you in trouble when you don't keep an appointment or fail to send a card for an important birthday. Your attention span is usually short and you are likely to disappear – both mentally and physically – from situations which become tedious. It is easy to tell when you've lost interest because your eyes just glaze over ...

The balancing act

What you need to learn in life is how to handle difficulties with a bit more tact, instead of doing what you normally do which is simply to bale out without a word. Be polite, and if you've made a commitment to do something, follow it through. You never know what you'll learn or find out. Take the trouble to explain yourself in more detail rather than skim through and hope for the best. Since you easily sniff out news, be careful about gossip. You're right in that some things are best left unsaid, and your great capacity for friendship will be all the better for your discretion.

The mirror effect

There's a hidden factor which many people overlook when they read about their sun sign – the *mirror effect*. Essentially, this is all about understanding your opposite sign. You see, your opposite sign is your shadow self – your other half. It complements and provides the missing links to your own character and nature. Your opposite sign is Sagittarius. Understanding and adopting some of the characteristics associated with people born under this sign will help you not only to become a much more rounded person, but also to improve the quality of your own life. For example, Sagittarius can show you how to:

- attract good fortune

- use your sense of humour to help others

- learn to be more philosophical in trying circumstances

But there's so much more that you can learn from Sagittarius, and throughout life you'll find that this sign holds the answers to many of the dilemmas and problems which you as a Gemini will experience. Gemini and Sagittarius are but two sides of the same coin, and together they make a formidable team. So, find out more by turning to your opposite sign and taking a leaf out of Sagittarius' book.

Your love nature

With razor-sharp Mercury as your planetary ruler, you're ever so quick at chat-up lines and full-on when it comes to charm. When you're flirting, your witty sense of humour and inventiveness give you an edge, but you do need to watch tactics.

Perhaps you could be more considerate about other people's feelings. You love spending time with friends who'll chat and your mobile/PC is usually red-hot getting the low-down on who's doing what or who's going out with whom. To you, variety is essential and commitment difficult, because there's so much to explore out there and so many people to meet. You need someone who understands your changeable nature and doesn't mind adapting to your adventurous way of life.

Cosmic combinations

Whom do you get on with best? Who sets your heart on fire, puts a smile on your lips and colour in your cheeks? Who brings you bliss and who gives you misery? Do you drive each other wild or up the wall? Check your love chart to find out.

Aries	great relate	❤❤❤❤
Taurus	no fun, no way	❤
Gemini	come fly with me	❤❤❤❤
Cancer	need a getaway clause	❤❤
Leo	fun and frolics	❤❤❤❤
Virgo	promising...	❤❤❤
Libra	soooo good	❤❤❤❤❤
Scorpio	too deep	❤
Sagittarius	attraction of opposites	❤❤❤❤
Capricorn	*very* unlikely	❤
Aquarius	harmonic souls	❤❤❤❤❤
Pisces	unreal moments	❤❤

❤ = no-no	❤❤❤❤ = cool couple
❤❤ = so-so	❤❤❤❤❤ = star match!
❤❤❤ = hang in there	

Talents and interests

You use your mind to solve riddles, puzzles, word games and, of course, crosswords. You use your hands creatively and your amazing dexterity is an asset in sports such as tennis, for example, or when playing cards or even tickling the ivories on a piano. You have excellent keyboard skills, too, and can understand computers like no one else. Because communication is so central to your life, you've always got a great joke to tell and are able to keep everyone amused and entertained for hours on end.

Study, work and career paths

You have a problem with your attention span – you know that, don't you? It's because you catch on so quickly and then you get bored, so you are easily sidetracked when you're doing your homework or studying for exams. One solution is to work in short bursts, but be specific and stick to a timetable and reward yourself at the end of each session by doing something you like. You're brilliant at finding clever short cuts, so when you're revising for exams write notes and reduce all your information to lists or ingenious mnemonics – handy little memory prompts.

Because as a sign Gemini has a restless spirit, it's advisable to get some early training and qualifications so you have something to fall back on when you decide to re-invent yourself in years to come. You're likely to have ambitions towards fame, and as an ideas person you usually think of something completely different with which to astound the world! Your communication skills are your greatest asset and your route to fame and fortune. You also have an ability to get on with

youngsters, which makes you a natural teacher. In fact, many Geminis gravitate to work in schools and universities. Don't forget, you're tremendously adaptable and inventive, and a great story-teller. And, given your imagination and your intuition, you could make a fine novelist, or work in the media as a journalist, foreign correspondent, newsreader or writer. Publishing, interpreting and translating are other big career draws for you.

Health and beauty

Geminis live on their nerves, so although they have vitality, they can use up energy fast and get stressed out. As a member of this sign, you need to learn to listen to what your body needs and understand when your nervous system is heading for overload. Make sure everything you eat and drink is absolutely fresh so as to give you maximum vitality. And because your mind works so fast, you need more sleep than the other signs to regenerate your system – a good excuse to leave a party early, should you wish to! The lungs, shoulders, arms and hands are ruled by Gemini and, as with the other Air signs, lots of fresh air is like medicine for your body. Practising meditation, yoga, t'ai chi or chi gong is particularly good for sustaining your body and for helping you to focus and concentrate. Health clubs are definitely your scene.

Female Geminis are usually attractive, often tall and slim with bright, expressive eyes. They tend to move quickly and neatly and are noticed for their rapid hand movements. Male Geminis tend to be above average in height, attractive, agile, and with eyes on a 'constant range mode', taking in everything and making mental notes. Both sexes like to be up to the minute

regarding news, fashion, and health and beauty products – but are prone to impulse buys.

Sign Associations

Birthstones: agate, tourmaline

Flower: lily-of-the-valley

Colours: pale yellow, white

Trees: ash, hazel

Birds: cockatoo, magpie

Animal: monkey

Foods: nuts

Countries: Belgium, Sardinia (Italy)

Body parts: lungs, shoulders, arms, hands

Cancer ♋
The Crab

23 June – 23 July
Ruling planet: the moon
Element: Water

Why you're lucky to be you!

Because you belong to the element Water, plus the fact that Cancer is the fourth sign and also occupies an important place in the wheel of the zodiac, you're one of the most protective and nurturing people in the universe. Your intuitive and imaginative nature makes you ultra sensitive so you are instantly able to tune in to other people's needs – and also to your own feelings. You're especially loved because you're so good at looking after folk, particularly children, friends and family. Good fortune follows you about, especially when shopping, bargain-hunting and doing deals.

You're a star because:

You're wonderfully sentimental, warm and caring. You're attached to your loved ones, to your home and to all the things you cherish that make your world a nice place in which to live. Whether you're the eldest or the youngest in your family, you would lay down your life to protect your brothers and sisters.

You treasure the past and, because so many Cancerians are among the world's most respected antiques collectors and historians, it is thanks to you and members of your sign that a good deal of our heritage is being preserved. Whether your passion is coins, stamps, beer mats or even carrier bags, carry on with your collections because today's ephemera are likely to become tomorrow's treasures and will prove to be worth their weight in gold for you in years to come.

Your special qualities

You're blessed with a formidable memory which serves you well – you rarely forget birthdays and other special occasions. And, of course, this comes in handy when you have to study or sit tests and exams. At home, you're happy to potter about the house and kitchen, and have probably enjoyed cooking since the first time you helped your mother bake a cake when you were a tiny tot. No matter how old you are, given your party skills, you have the ability to create enjoyment for everyone, especially when you're entertaining your family and close friends. What's more, wherever you go you are able to turn the meanest dwelling into a bright, cosy and pleasant home.

However...

You can be hugely vulnerable and overemotional, often creating your own 'soap opera' when things have gone wrong. It's not that you're not practical – you are; it's just that of all the signs Cancerians are most easily moved to tears by sad things such as endings, injuries and injustice. For you, a good cry is a valuable way of releasing tension, but you must be careful that it doesn't become tears with everything just to get your own way! You can become obsessive about a person, a group, the

environment, a piece of music – anything that grabs your feelings – and end up emotionally drained. And then, of course, there's that long memory of yours that makes it so difficult for you to forgive and forget.

The balancing act

Because a natural shrewdness and a strong link to tradition are in your very genes, you soon learn what your values are and what makes you feel secure. The art of successfully dealing with emotions lies in learning to detach – but it is not always clear how to do this. The answer is to get things in perspective and find a practical solution to whatever is bothering you. Sometimes you tend to worry too much about other people, taking their problems onto your own shoulders. Your caring nature is wonderful, but if something's not your direct problem you must ask yourself whether you should get involved. Perhaps a big lesson for you to learn in life is to care for yourself first so that you are in a better position to help others.

The mirror effect

There's a hidden factor which many people overlook when they read about their sun sign – the *mirror effect*. Essentially, this is all about understanding your opposite sign. You see, your opposite sign is your shadow self – your other half. It complements and provides the missing links to your own character and nature. Your opposite sign is Capricorn. Understanding and adopting some of the characteristics associated with people born under this sign will help you not only to become a much more rounded person, but also to attract more good fortune into your own life. For example, Capricorn can show you how to:

- make your dreams come true
- improve your way of working
- build your inner strengths

But there's so much more that you can learn from Capricorn, and throughout life you'll find that this sign holds the answers to many of the dilemmas and problems which you as a Cancerian will experience. Cancer and Capricorn are but two sides of the same coin, and together they make a formidable team. So, find out more by turning to your opposite sign and taking a leaf out of Capricorn's book.

Your love nature

With the moon as your planetary ruler, you can't help but be a true romantic. However, you can be a touch elusive in matters of the heart because you're fundamentally shy. And you're even more cautious if you've been through a break-up with someone, because you know how deep your feelings can go. Emotionally, your moods can go up and down and in and out like the tides. Keep track of the lunar cycles because you'll find your moods are influenced by the moon, especially the full moon and the eclipses. Watching a romantic film or reading love stories in the warmth of your home is reassuring not only to female Cancerians, but to males too.

Cosmic combinations

Whom do you get on with best? Who sets your heart on fire, puts a smile on your lips and colour in your cheeks? Who brings you bliss and who gives you misery? Do you drive each other wild or up the wall? Check your love chart to find out.

Aries	will burn you dry	♥
Taurus	in tune	♥♥♥♥
Gemini	futile logic	♥
Cancer	deep harmony	♥♥♥♥♥
Leo	too theatrical?	♥♥♥
Virgo	hidden undercurrents	♥♥♥♥
Libra	hard work	♥
Scorpio	soul-deep	♥♥♥♥♥
Sagittarius	insensitive	♥♥
Capricorn	attraction of opposites	♥♥♥♥
Aquarius	possibly intriguing	♥♥
Pisces	oceanic bliss	♥♥♥♥♥

♥ = no-no   ♥♥♥♥ = cool couple
♥♥ = so-so   ♥♥♥♥♥ = star match!
♥♥♥ = hang in there

Talents and interests

Because of your sign's association with history and the past, many Cancerians delve into archaeology, ancient artefacts and historical costume – in fact any area which can reveal fascinating information about the environment and our ancestors. Museums, art galleries and antiques feed this interest, and your curiosity about the past means that you find viewing stately

homes absolutely fascinating. You're 'at home' in natural surroundings such as gardens and woods, and especially places near water. With your green fingers, you can successfully grow and nurture plants where others fail. At any age, being a Cancerian means you will always be a 'water baby', enjoying sports such as swimming, surfing, snorkelling and diving – or just messing about in boats. And if you can't get to the seaside, never mind, a long soak in the bath will do nicely!

Study, work and career paths

You have an excellent retentive memory – indeed, perhaps one of the longest memories in the entire zodiac! So you shouldn't be too bad at remembering facts and figures, historical dates and important names, which of course comes in handy when revising for exams. But, as a general rule, when you're studying, writing up essays or assignments, try to be as direct as possible and train yourself to *answer the question*. All too often you go round in circles before getting to the point. So, if you want to get better grades, cut the waffle and get to the core of your answer fast!

Just like the crab that symbolises your sign, you never take a direct approach but prefer to sneak in sideways. And in many ways this applies to the way you work. For a start, your mind takes a roundabout route when processing any information – even when doing a simple calculation you seem to go round the houses in order to arrive at the correct answer. It is the same with your career. It may take you several years and some false starts doing this and that before you find your true niche in life. Because of your nature, you may find dealing in antiques or working as an archaeologist or museum curator most satis-

fying. A career in and around water would also please. Boat-building, sailing, fishing or being a lifeguard, for example, come to mind. Nursing and caring, too, suit the gentler side of the Cancerian nature. Careers in interior design or the hotel or catering trade, as well as in market gardening or horticulture, are also ideal for members of your sign.

Health and beauty

The sign Cancer rules the chest and stomach, areas which get affected when you're emotionally upset – manifesting in indigestion and stomach upsets, for example. How you feel dictates the state of your health, and when you have emotional problems you'll notice you get thoroughly run down as your immune system becomes weakened. Having said that, you can take comfort in the fact that, as a Cancerian, you're generally tough and recover from illness quicker than many other signs.

Female Cancerians usually have a round face with a delicate milky complexion and expressive eyes. They in particular tend to have a problem with keeping their weight constant – which for all of us is a nuisance because it fluctuates as a result of storing and releasing water – and choosing clothes can be a bit of a bugbear. Male Cancerians have a tendency to get chubby, especially later in life. But both males and females have devastating smiles that can take your breath away. Swimming is great for both relaxation and exercise for all members of this sign. An occasional spell of solitude in the countryside also helps to calm the spirit and recharge the batteries. Drinking plenty of pure water is the best medicine for Cancerians. Bath or shower products as well as herbal and mud treatments are excellent beauty buys and are appreciated by Crabs of all ages.

Lucky Stars

Sign Associations

Birthstone: moonstone

Flower: water lily

Colour: silver

Tree: willow

Bird: owl

Animals: cat, crab

Foods: shellfish, watermelon

Countries: Canada, USA, the Netherlands

Body parts: chest, stomach, breasts

Leo ♌
The Lion

24 July – 23 August
Ruling planet: the sun
Element: Fire

Why you're lucky to be you!

Belonging as you do to the fifth sign of the zodiac, you come across as a warm individual with a wonderfully colourful, fiery and vital nature. You love a bit of drama, but that's because you're essentially creative and a true actor at heart. Sometimes you can be over the top – there isn't a Leo alive who doesn't crave to be the centre of attention. But you were born with sunshine in your soul and a love of life that infects everyone you meet with happiness. You're a natural extrovert with a magical ability to inspire everyone with your hope, laughter and delight.

You're a star because:

You're a natural celebrity. You're regal and attractive, charming, glossy, vibrant and full of life. You're fiercely independent, yet loyal and courageous. And you're generous and big-hearted,

too. You like to be liked and love to be loved and, like all stars of stage and screen, you thrive on attention. You've got built-in sex appeal and a magnetic personality that draws admirers to your side. Once you've made up your mind about something, nothing will stop you reaching your goal.

Your special qualities

Achieving success in some area of your life is important to you, so luckily you are endowed with enough willpower to come out on top. One of your greatest assets is your optimism and sheer love of life, and it is this, incidentally, that gives you the edge when times are hard. Even your sense of humour can come to your rescue and save the day. Like the lion that rules your sign, you're noted for your courage. Your kindness means that you're always prepared to help others in need. You're a great organiser and especially good with young children.

However...

You are a great big show-off. Your dramatic and dominating ways can sometimes be overwhelming. And that legendary pride of yours makes you stubborn and often prevents you from being able to admit you're wrong. You can be hugely demanding and dogmatic, wanting everyone to do things your way, and when they don't or won't it's not unusual for you to fly into a rage. Yes, your temper can badly let you down and spoil so many of your good qualities. Saying you're sorry may be difficult for you, but is a lesson well worth learning.

The balancing act

It's vital that you see the other person's point of view if you are to make the big time in anything that you do. Fire signs, as we

know, are 'doers'; they tend not to hang around planning and thinking but prefer the challenge of pitching themselves into the action. You, more than all the other signs, need the support of the 'group', and one way to be sure you get the loyal followers you require is to cultivate a little more patience and diplomacy. Accepting that other people might have good ideas and positive input would help to oil the wheels and make the difference between a wise leader and a dictator.

The mirror effect

There's a hidden factor which many people overlook when they read about their sun sign – the *mirror effect*. Essentially, this is all about understanding your opposite sign. You see, your opposite sign is your shadow self – your other half. It complements and provides the missing links to your own character and nature. Your opposite sign is Aquarius. Understanding and adopting some of the characteristics associated with people born under this sign will help you not only to become a much more rounded person, but also to attract more good fortune into your own life. For example, Aquarius can show you how to:

- gain a unique, global view of life
- dream up original and improving ideas
- find compassion in your heart

But there's so much more that you can learn from Aquarius, and throughout life you'll find that this sign holds the answers to many of the dilemmas and problems which you as a Leo will experience. Leo and Aquarius are but two sides of the same coin and together they make a formidable team. So, find out more by turning to your opposite sign and taking a leaf out of Aquarius' book.

Your love nature

Yours is a very romantic and affectionate sign, and this does indeed describe your loving nature. But, remember, you're a lion and, just like that exotic creature, when you set your sights on someone you fancy, you move in purposefully and relentlessly for the 'kill'. You possess a magnetic sexuality and, when in love, you're loyal and honest. In relationships, you respond best to someone who can be equally open-hearted. You do tend to dominate a partnership, but you thrive with someone who will now and then present you with a challenge. After all, life would be awfully boring if you always got your own way, wouldn't it?

Cosmic combinations

Whom do you get on with best? Who sets your heart on fire, puts a smile on your lips and colour in your cheeks? Who brings you bliss and who gives you misery? Do you drive each other wild or up the wall? Check your love chart to find out.

Lucky Stars

Aries	terrific!	❤❤❤❤❤
Taurus	earthy sensuality	❤❤❤
Gemini	stimulating	❤❤❤❤
Cancer	too steamy?	❤❤❤
Leo	passion mates	❤❤❤❤❤
Virgo	hmm ... not really	❤
Libra	romantic interlude	❤❤❤
Scorpio	deep challenge	❤❤❤❤
Sagittarius	pure adventure!	❤❤❤❤❤
Capricorn	promising	❤❤❤
Aquarius	attraction of opposites	❤❤❤❤
Pisces	drenching	❤❤❤

❤ = no-no   ❤❤❤❤ = cool couple

❤❤ = so-so   ❤❤❤❤❤ = star match!

❤❤❤ = hang in there

Talents and interests

Your love of life needs expression, so the dramatic arts, dance and show-biz are in your blood. Sporting activities are also high on your list, and you get on well with people of all ages. Your talent for fashion and design is usually obvious – from what you wear, the way you live and how you decorate your room (with jazzy posters and always with an eye for luxury). You like to lounge about in comfort and you're good at entertaining and throwing parties. Better still, you love going out and having fun.

Study, work and career paths

Be honest, you can be a tad lazy sometimes, leaving your homework and course assignments right up until the deadline. Then there's a mad rush, which might involve phoning your best friend for the answers or staying up late to get the work done. Get smart. You know how you shine when you get good marks, how you love the sound of clapping and congratulations when you come top of the class. Remember that great feeling and use it as an incentive. If you apply yourself, work harder and a little more consistently, there's no reason why you shouldn't get excellent grades all the time and then, of course, you can enjoy all the praise that goes with your wonderful achievement.

As a Leo, your artistic talents can lead you to art college or drama school. You're also hugely creative, so any career where you can use your imagination would suit you. Apart from the media, advertising and PR, the worlds of design, the beauty business and fashion are also your scene. You do like to be a leader and to carry responsibility, so think about a possible career in the teaching profession, in theatre or stage management, or even in youth work.

Health and beauty

Your ruler is the sun, which represents your life battery. Because you're so vital and full of energy most of the time, you have a tendency to take your health for granted. You're a bit of a party animal who likes to burn the candle at both ends, so you'll run the risk of burn-out if you're not careful. Leo rules the heart and the spine and these are the areas of the body you should treat with extra respect and care. High blood pressure can

become a problem for Leos later on in life. Back strengthening exercises, dance movements, yoga and the martial arts will help you to maintain a good upright posture. However, your general strong constitution keeps the minor bugs at bay and enables you to recovery quickly from illness.

Female Leos characteristically have a mane of beautiful hair and a slim, sensuous body. Male Leos, too, tend to have thick, wavy or curly hair, a broad back and good, strong muscles. You adore beauty and hair care products, and when purchasing them you like to buy only the best, often designer brands.

Sign Associations

Birthstone: ruby

Flower: sunflower

Colours: gold, sun yellow

Tree: birch

Bird: swan

Animals: lion, all cats

Foods: all rich flavours

Countries: France, Italy

Body parts: heart, spine

Virgo ♍
The Maiden

24 August – 23 September
Ruling planet: Mercury
Element: Earth

Why you're lucky to be you!

You're clever and organised and have a wonderful gift for being able to see a situation from every angle. Others may get confused and find they can't see 'the wood for the trees', but not you! You're eagle-eyed and can spot the minutest detail at 50 metres. You're brilliant when it comes to making decisions because you instantly recognise the how, what, when, where and why of every question. You are neat and methodical, and no one can beat your powers of analysis and your gift for practical thinking.

You're a star because:

You're so cool. You may come across as quiet and unassuming, perhaps even shy sometimes, but it's all registering and going on deep inside that brilliant mind of yours. You don't miss a trick. Details matter to you so you're constantly thinking,

watching and assessing everyone you meet and everything that's going on. Helpful and versatile, you're blessed with a sympathetic nature, and because your common sense is so rock solid, friends always come to you first for advice.

Your special qualities

All Virgos have sharp insight – that wonderful ability to get to the nitty-gritty of things quicker than a streak of lightning. So nothing gets past you. You can spot a liar in the blink of an eye. And your humour! It is so dry and witty that you can have friends in stitches all night long. Because you can home in on detail so easily, it means you're a terrific student, able to get straight As in research projects and exams. You have a precise sense of style which comes out in practical and creative ways – in your art, in projects with wood and fabrics, and in gardening. Yes, you have green fingers, too.

However...

You're fussy and fastidious. You're also a bit of a worrier. That's mainly because you tend to lack self-confidence and you're critical of yourself and your abilities. The problem is,

you're a perfectionist, so no matter how well you do a job you end up dwelling on the mistakes, on the blemishes and the faults, instead of feeling satisfied with the good work you've done. In your mind, it could always be better. And again, it's that fine eye for picking up on details that has earned you the reputation of being downright picky. Your critical nature and habit of dryly pointing out other people's failings to them can be your downfall.

The balancing act

Finding ways to relax and loosen up is a good start. Accepting that no one, including yourself, is perfect is a big step, too. You can be rather blunt, especially when expressing your disapproval, so learning to be more tactful when dealing with others would certainly help to smooth your relationships. Remember, it's often kinder to leave things unsaid than to say something negative. Develop your imagination – your pragmatic approach to life can be rather limiting and narrow. So, go on, unleash those fantasies and blow your cares away.

The mirror effect

There's a hidden factor which many people overlook when they read about their sun sign – the *mirror effect*. Essentially, this is all about understanding your opposite sign. You see, your opposite sign is your shadow self – your other half. It complements and provides the missing links to your own character and nature. Your opposite sign is Pisces. Understanding and adopting some of the characteristics associated with people born under this sign will help you not only to become a much more rounded person, but also to attract more good fortune into your own life. For example, Pisces can show you how to:

- *really* unwind and relax
- develop your romantic nature
- dream your dreams awake

But there's so much more that you can learn from Pisces, and throughout life you'll find that this sign holds the answers to many of the dilemmas and problems which you as a Virgo will experience. Virgo and Pisces are but two sides of the same coin, and together they make a formidable team. So, find out more by turning to your opposite sign and taking a leaf out of Pisces' book.

Your love nature

You have a hidden, romantic quality which comes out when you find someone really special. That's when your lovely, caring side truly blossoms. Because of Virgo shyness, however, you need to get to know someone very well before you become involved romantically. So for you, love can grow out of friendship. You're not given to sentimentality or to cooing-and-billing because your head rules your heart, so of all the signs you find it the easiest to recover from a break-up. You don't like boorish behaviour or lewd remarks – you have a very pure heart, you see. When you do fall in love, you're usually faithful and committed and you expect the same from your partner in return.

Cosmic combinations

Whom do you get on with best? Who sets your heart on fire, puts a smile on your lips and colour in your cheeks? Who brings you bliss and who gives you misery? Do you drive each other wild or up the wall? Check your love chart to find out.

Aries	thoughtless	❤❤
Taurus	reliable comfort	❤❤❤❤❤
Gemini	on and off	❤❤❤
Cancer	comfortable	❤❤❤❤
Leo	abrasive	❤
Virgo	soul-mates	❤❤❤❤❤
Libra	off balance	❤
Scorpio	fascinating	❤❤❤❤
Sagittarius	unreal	❤
Capricorn	winning ways	❤❤❤❤❤
Aquarius	unpredictable	❤❤
Pisces	attraction of opposites	❤❤❤❤

❤ = no-no   ❤❤❤❤ = cool couple
❤❤ = so-so   ❤❤❤❤❤ = star match!
❤❤❤ = hang in there

Talents and interests

As an Earth sign you're in touch with the needs of everything
and everyone around you. Being out in the open countryside is
good for you, and you're good for it, too, because as well as
having a 'green' mind which can tune in to Nature, you also
appreciate issues that affect the environment, including animals and their welfare. Food and health are also topics that
fascinate you. You seem to have an instinctive awareness of
when your body needs vitamins. You're very keen on a healthy
diet with natural or fresh foods and you can be relied upon to
know where to find the best health food shops in town. You're
clever and thrifty with money. You learn quickly and have a
special ability to teach and to impart knowledge to others.

Study, work and career paths

Typically, Virgos tend to have the neatest exercise books in the whole class, so if you're true to your sign you'll be a teacher's dream. Like the other two Earth signs, you work diligently, do your homework regularly and hand your assignments in on time. But when it comes to exams you can be a bit of a worrier, anxious that you won't get the grades. So learning a few relaxation exercises would come in handy. Another good tip is to get your hands on a couple of 'how to pass exams with flying colours' books. Study them, learn exam techniques and you'll have it all sewn up.

Because you're such an earnest and committed sort of person, you see work more as a vocation than a means of survival. Because you're one of life's carers you'll probably gravitate to one of those occupations that serve mankind, such as teaching or medicine. One way or another, you'll be involved in 'serving others', but in a truly fulfilling kind of way. Members of your sign are often drawn to the health service and make fine doctors and nurses – or vets. Your critical talents also excel in occupations that involve analysis or scientific research. Since you're interested in food, you may be happy to work as a dietician or nutritionist. Writing, lecturing, journalism or literary criticism would also suit you. Practical jobs such as craft-work or gardening, where you can roll up your sleeves and get down to business, would bring great satisfaction – as would a career in accountancy or computer technology.

Health and beauty

Healthy habits are top of the Virgo list, so you can be very choosy about food and critical of quality when eating out. The

truth is, you know you have a delicate and sensitive constitution and a nervous system which can easily overload into electrical hum. Calming activities such as meditation and yoga suit you and are your best medicine. However, you are fascinated with herbal remedies, complementary medicine and medical dictionaries, and you must be careful not to get too carried away with pills and potions.

Female Virgos usually have a neat look about them, with a refined body and a well-cut head of hair. They are often noted for their attractive features, but must learn to relax or their faces will show a certain tenseness about the eyes and jaw line. For the same reason, male Virgos have a habit of appearing permanently preoccupied. Their bodies tend to be lean and well proportioned.

Sign Associations

Birthstones: sardonyx, peridot

Flowers: lavender, buttercup

Colours: green, brown

Tree: elder

Bird: stork

Animal: fox

Foods: corn, rice

Countries: Turkey, Greece, Brazil

Body parts: digestive system, intestines

Libra ♎
The Scales

24 September – 23 October
Ruling planet: Venus
Element: Air

Why you're lucky to be you!

You're likeable and easy-going and you attract people because you're co-operative with others and like to share your time and thoughts with them. In fact, your affable nature makes you everybody's friend. Because you hate to hurt people's feelings, you've got tact and diplomacy off to a fine art. Always seemingly up to date, you have a style that's so classic, it never goes out of fashion. You're a natural when it comes to beauty and taste. You have great manners and always know the right things to say.

You're a star because:

You're so charming and everyone wants to be with you. You have exquisite taste, always appearing cool and unruffled even in the most frantic situations. Quality rather than quantity is what you go for – and it shows! You're thoughtful, too, cul-

tured and refined. All in all, you could be described as a classy piece of work. You're up-market and, whether it's food, fashion or things to make life pleasant, you go for the best that money can buy. In every way, you're star quality through and through.

Your special qualities

First and foremost, you're a good listener and a truly sympathetic friend. You love helping out, organising parties and get-togethers. You're not too fond of very loud music, though, and you like everyone to be pleasant and everything to run smoothly. But when your friends come round you know how to make sure they relax and have a good time. You're very generous in all kinds of ways and are happy to lend out things – clothes, accessories or books. And you're wonderful at giving good, balanced advice. If your friends ever need an impartial judgement, you're the first person they think of coming to.

However...

You find it ever so difficult to make decisions. To be honest, you're a bit of fence-sitter; so eager are you not to fall out with anyone that you prefer not to take sides – which can be rather frustrating. You also find it impossible to commit yourself. Should you go with this sweetheart or possibly that one? Well, this one is good-looking, but that one is rich. Decisions, decisions. You spend so long umming and ahhing that you risk losing out all together. Because looks are so important to you, you'll take up with someone just for their appearance rather than for their personality. This suggests that, despite all your refinement, you can be a bit shallow.

The balancing act

Since you're the sign of the Scales you know all about the difficulties of trying to keep everything and everyone in balance and in harmony. You have a tendency to live other people's lives and to take their problems personally. This is something you must learn not to do. You should also try to train yourself not to turn things over and over and over in your mind. A decision – any decision – is better than no decision at all. It's certainly better than going over the same ground day after day for fear of making a mistake. Learn to let go. If things get on

top of you, go for a walk, take some exercise, join in a sport. And, above all else, stop feeling so guilty!

The mirror effect

There's a hidden factor which many people overlook when they read about their sun sign – the *mirror effect*. Essentially, this is all about understanding your opposite sign. You see, your opposite sign is your shadow self – your other half. It complements and provides the missing links to your own character and nature. Your opposite sign is Aries. Understanding and adopting some of the characteristics associated with people born under this sign will help you not only to become a much more rounded person, but also to attract more good fortune

into your own life. For example, Aries can show you how to:

- make quick decisions
- become more self-reliant
- improve your health and finances and find greater happiness

But there's so much more that you can learn from Aries, and throughout life you'll find that this sign holds the answers to many of the dilemmas and problems which you as a Libran will experience. Libra and Aries are but two sides of the same coin, and together they make a formidable team. So, find out more by turning to your opposite sign and taking a leaf out of Aries' book.

Your love nature

With Venus as your ruling planet, you love to be loved. But you're a romantic and all too often you tend just to be in love with the notion of being in love rather than have true feelings for the person you're with. This can happen when you're flattered by attention and rush into a relationship without really thinking about what it means. However, the sign Libra rules relationships, so you're never happier than when part of a twosome. You hate being alone and in truth need a good-looking, supportive and loving companion by your side.

Cosmic combinations

Whom do you get on with best? Who sets your heart on fire, puts a smile on your lips and colour in your cheeks? Who brings you bliss and who gives you misery? Do you drive each other wild or up the wall? Check your love chart to find out.

Aries	blending of opposites	❤❤❤❤
Taurus	occasionally	❤❤❤
Gemini	just delightful!	❤❤❤❤❤
Cancer	wet sponge	❤
Leo	sparky, clashy	❤❤
Virgo	too exacting	❤❤
Libra	keep your balance!	❤❤❤❤
Scorpio	trial run?	❤❤❤
Sagittarius	a brief diversion	❤❤❤
Capricorn	you're joking!	❤
Aquarius	just bliss	❤❤❤❤❤
Pisces	flow gently, chill out	❤❤❤

❤ = no-no   ❤❤❤❤ = cool couple

❤❤ = so-so   ❤❤❤❤❤ = star match!

❤❤❤ = hang in there

Talents and interests

Your charm and easy-going nature give you the edge in dealing with people of all ages. Moreover, you have an intelligent approach which can solve problems and succeed where others fear to tread. You have a discerning eye for perspective, colour and style, so you're invaluable when it comes to giving advice on fashion and style. You enjoy music and are talented yourself, so probably play an instrument. Indeed, many Librans are talented dancers, singers or musicians. You have the best eye in town for designer labels and your favourite passion in the whole world has to be retail therapy!

Lucky Stars

Study, work and career paths

When it comes to studying, indecision can be your main bug-bear – as in all other aspects of your life. Should you start with this subject, answer that question, read this book now or leave everything until another day? What you need is a study buddy – someone you can bat ideas about with. You can also work together on projects and, when it comes to exams, you can take turns at testing each other. Remember, too, that it's difficult to concentrate in a grotty room, so tidy up and make your study environment as pleasant and congenial as possible. Hang posters on the wall, put flowers in a vase, open the window and let in the fresh air. A pleasant atmosphere is the best food for your brain.

You don't like blood and gore and were not born to fetch and carry for others. The fact is, you don't like getting your hands dirty so any job that requires manual labour is not really your scene at all. Nor are you at your best in dirty, unpleasant sur-roundings. You're an intellectual really, and perhaps best described as a 'white collar worker'. The areas in which you excel include the music business, fashion, the theatre, and jew-ellery design. You could become a fine architect, a diplomat or a lawyer. The beauty industry also attracts you, and because often you're very elegant, you could grace the catwalk as a model or appear on the cover of glossy magazines.

Health and beauty

Because everything about you involves the notion of balance, it's important that you make sure your mind and body are always in perfect harmony. Yoga, t'ai chi, dance, movement, meditation and gymnastics are ways of de-stressing and main-

taining body health for you. Games such as tennis are ideal, and so is walking – which is not too strenuous for a Libra like yourself! Your sign is associated with the liver and kidneys, so you need to drink lots of water on a daily basis to keep your system well flushed and free from toxins. A light diet that avoids rich foods is also best for you.

As a rule, female Librans are attractive and feminine and know how to move with grace. More often than not they are blonde or have reddish hair. Male Librans tend to have a slender body structure. They are graceful movers with serene, attractive faces. Librans of both sexes are fussy about their appearance and like quality gear – they take ages getting ready to go out! Only the best, luxury beauty products with expensive, heavenly scents will do for the members of this sign.

Sign Associations

Birthstones: opal, rose quartz

Flowers: sweet pea, violet

Colours: pale pink, pale blue

Trees: fig, vine

Bird: dove

Animal: dolphin

Foods: milk, honey

Countries: Austria, China, Tibet

Body parts: kidneys, liver

Scorpio ♏
The Scorpion

24 October – 22 November
Ruling planets: Pluto, Mars
Element: Water

Why you're lucky to be you!

If you're a Scorpio, you belong to the most mystical and powerful sign of the zodiac. As a member of this clan, you have a
reputation for being sexy and magnetically attractive. There's
something mysterious about you, something deep and unfath-
omable that draws people to you, wanting to know your
secrets. For you are secretive, and it's that very quiet, cool
charm of yours that others find so compelling. And it's this
same quality that enables you to you get things done without
anyone even noticing. You're a terrific detective with a mind
that delights in research and uncovering hidden things. You
have a penetrating gaze that seems to bore through to a
person's very soul – it can be unnerving but just adds to your
fascinating allure.

Lucky Stars

You're a star because:

You are simply the ultimate in cool. Intensely charismatic, strong, focused and determined, you're a class apart from the rest, setting your own style and your own agenda. You don't suffer fools gladly, and you have a brilliant knack for coming up with just the right 'put down' lines that can cut to the quick when required. This, of course, is that famous sting in the Scorpion's tail which warns others to mess with you at their peril! You attract a great number of loyal friends who admire your strength and integrity.

Your special qualities

You're gifted with a brilliant imagination which can flourish in many artistic and creative ways. But it's your probing mind that's your greatest asset. That, and your formidable powers of intuition. Some would even say that you're psychic because you have an uncanny ability to penetrate and pick up on other people's thoughts. Very often, you just seem to *know* about things. Perhaps that's because you adore gathering and storing information and have mental files in your head about things which no one would even suspect. Persistent and determined, you possess tremendous staying power and insist on seeing a plan or project right through to the bitter end.

However...

You can be obsessive, not recognising when to give up. And downright manipulative, too. But it's jealousy that's your biggest hang-up. You're tremendously loyal yourself and you expect others to be, too. When someone lets you down, upsets you or crosses you (especially in love), your instinctive reaction

is to get even. Sometimes you respond immediately and lethally with that deadly sting of yours, but at other times you silently seethe with resentment and plan your revenge with minute precision. It may take you some time – even years – to strike, but strike back you will. Oh yes you will, because, you see, a Scorpio *never forgives or forgets*!

The balancing act

More self-critical than most signs, you find it quite difficult to maintain a balance since you have such a sensitive inner core. The keyword for you to remember is *creativity*. When you feel things are getting heavy or your emotions are taking you over, get away from everything – go for a jog, a cycle ride or get over to the gym to let off steam. Sport and exercise are what you need to release those endorphins – the hormones that change our mood and make us feel happy. Get stuck into a creative project, do some research, give yourself a mission to keep your mind busy and interested in something worthwhile.

The mirror effect

There's a hidden factor which many people overlook when they read about their sun sign – the *mirror effect*. Essentially, this is all about understanding your opposite sign. You see, your opposite sign is your shadow self – your other half. It complements and provides the missing links to your own character and nature. Your opposite sign is Taurus. Understanding and adopting some of the characteristics associated with people born under this sign will help you not only to become a much more rounded person, but also to attract more good fortune into your own life. For example, Taurus can show you how to:

- find emotional and material security and contentment
- love, spoil and enjoy yourself
- organise yourself and become practically efficient

But there's so much more that you can learn from Taurus, and throughout life you'll find that this sign holds the answers to many of the dilemmas and problems which you as a Scorpio will experience. Scorpio and Taurus are but two sides of the same coin, and together they make a formidable team. So, find out more by turning to your opposite sign and taking a leaf out of Taurus' book.

Your love nature

Well, it's *intense and magnetic*! It's all or nothing for you. When you fall for someone, you pour everything into that relationship: body, mind and spirit – the lot. As far as you're concerned, couples should be faithful and loyal to each other, so when you give your heart, that's a firm commitment and it's for keeps.

You're doggedly persistent and when you fancy someone, you generally won't give up until you have conquered that person. (In truth, you love the chase.) You are immensely passionate and when it comes to loving someone, you're full-on.

Cosmic combinations

Whom do you get on with best? Who sets your heart on fire, puts a smile on your lips and colour in your cheeks? Who brings you bliss and who gives you misery? Do you drive each other wild or up the wall? Check your love chart to find out.

Aries	challenging passion	♥♥♥♥
Taurus	attraction of opposites	♥♥♥♥
Gemini	impossible	♥
Cancer	soul connection	♥♥♥♥♥
Leo	could be fun	♥♥♥
Virgo	supportive warmth	♥♥♥
Libra	nothing serious	♥♥
Scorpio	madly, deeply	♥♥♥♥♥
Sagittarius	fun diversion	♥♥
Capricorn	earthy devotion	♥♥♥♥
Aquarius	worth investigating	♥♥♥
Pisces	deeply romantic	♥♥♥♥♥

♥ = no-no   ♥♥♥♥ = cool couple

♥♥ = so-so   ♥♥♥♥♥ = star match!

♥♥♥ = hang in there

Talents and interests

Your special talent is having the courage and discipline to pursue the unusual and the mysterious. You enjoy all kinds of weird and wonderful research. Myths, legends, past civilisations, ancient religions, DNA, ghost hunting, graves – anything in fact that's out of the ordinary or where a greater truth is hidden and needs to be uncovered. You like to do your own

thing and be your own person, so working intensely in isolation or with a small team is ideal. You're a self-starter with projects and ambitions, and you're quite capable of re-inventing yourself at various intervals throughout your life.

Study, work and career paths

As long as you can do your own research, you'll spend hours and hours engrossed in your studies. But whether you like studying at all rather depends on whether you get on with the teachers or not. If you do, you'll be an A-grade student. If you don't, you won't want to bother. Hopefully, you'll find a subject area, such as science, which fascinates you, or a teacher with whom you can bond or develop an understanding. The important thing for you is to knuckle down and get through your school work so you can gain grades that will be good enough to give you the opportunity to go on to bigger and better things. Because you have an investigative mind, a university course would be just up your street.

As a Scorpio, you need to get emotional satisfaction from whatever job you do. It may take a while to find an area that suits you, but once the work *feels* right, you'll focus and dedicate yourself to that career. Your investigative mind would naturally take you into the police force, where you would soon rise to the rank of detective. Your fascination for the macabre opens up a whole panoply of suitable careers – forensic science, pathology or undertaking, for example. And because you like to probe the inner workings of the mind and body, you could be drawn to psychology, psychiatry, surgery or medical research. Alternatively, you'd make an astute banker or financial advisor.

Health and beauty

Because you have such powerful and dominating energies, you really do need regular exercise to keep your mind and body healthy, balanced and toned. Martial arts, kick boxing and contact sports are ideal for you. So is swimming, working out in the gym, cycling and circuit training. Think, too, about yoga and meditation, very useful activities to calm those seething emotions of yours. You like to cultivate an outward image that is both attractive and has panache, so you tend to wear a lot of dark colours.

Female Scorpios are known for their sexy, curvy bodies, strong-featured faces, appealing eyes and flowing, dark, wavy hair. You can tell a male Scorpio because he has magnetic eyes, abundant dark hair and, often, thick eyebrows. His body tends to be strong with a broad chest and, oh yes, don't forget that unmissable telltale sign – he simply oozes sex appeal!

Sign Associations

Birthstones: jasper, bloodstone, topaz

Flower: amaryllis

Colours: dark red, black

Trees: pine, blackthorn

Birds: eagle, dove

Animals: snake, scorpion

Foods: bean, leek, spicy food

Countries: Egypt, Norway, Algeria

Body parts: sex organs, bladder, large intestine

Sagittarius ↗
The Archer

23 November – 21 December
Ruling planet: Jupiter
Element: Fire

Why you're lucky to be you!

Because your sign is ruled by the planet Jupiter, you are considered the most fortunate member of the zodiac. You see, not only is Jupiter the most jovial of the planets, endowing you with a jolly, happy-go-lucky nature, but it also brings you lots of lucky opportunities and fun times throughout your life. Your sign is associated with teaching and travel, so being a Sagittarian means that you have the chance to expand your knowledge and your vistas both mentally and physically. There's no doubt about it – you're going places, and how!

You're a star because:

You have an open, honest, fun-loving personality and can't help attracting friends and admirers wherever you go. You're idealistic and an extrovert with a great sense of humour. Optimistic and enthusiastic, you bring cheer to everyone you

meet. Like your symbolic ruler, the centaur, you gallop through life, absorbing every kind of experience from different cultures and religions. You're truly cosmopolitan and may find yourself working or settling in a foreign country. An eternal student and wise philosopher, you enjoy reading and thinking and always have an amusing story or anecdote to tell. You're a party person with a natural gift for brightening up even the dullest of days.

Your special qualities

Easy-going and versatile, you have no trouble adapting to any situation or fitting in with any crowd. You're generous to a fault, giving away money and possessions to those who are in greater need than you. Indeed, many of the world's philanthropists are members of your sign. You have a fascination for the written and spoken word and a quick grasp of foreign languages. You're intuitive, too, and have an uncanny knack of somehow hitting the nail on the head with your remarks. Curious, restless, energetic and active, you excel at games and team sports of all kinds.

However...

You can be thoroughly tactless and although you don't mean to hurt anyone with your throw-away remarks, they can really upset those who are more sensitive than you. You're a bit of a larger-than-life sort of character and can sometimes exaggerate

(even boast) in order to get your point across. Since you work by instinct and very spontaneously, you tend to gloss over details, taking in the bigger picture, always looking to the furthest horizon and consequently missing what's going on under your very nose. You're untidy and tend to spread everything around you – books, clothes and stuff you're using, or that you used last week or last month! You get so carried away with excitement for the next project that you often have trouble completing the one that you're working on now.

The balancing act

It's obvious that learning to *discriminate* – making sensible choices and decisions – is the 'Big Balancing Act' for you, Sagittarius. You can spend far too much time creating an effect for other people while neglecting your own responsibilities and your own life! You owe it to yourself to get your career sorted, possibly through training or higher education, so that you can lay down a structure around which you can work and develop your skills. Learning to become more organised and efficient is the way to achieve your aims and find success.

The mirror effect

There's a hidden factor which many people overlook when they read about their sun sign – the *mirror effect*. Essentially, this is all about understanding your opposite sign. You see, your opposite sign is your shadow self – your other half. It complements and provides the missing links to your own character and nature. Your opposite sign is Gemini. Understanding and adopting some of the characteristics associated with people born under this sign will help you not only to become a much more rounded person, but also to attract more good fortune

into your own life. For example, Gemini can show you how to:

- communicate better with people
- make better use of your imagination
- become more practical and develop attention to detail

But there's so much more that you can learn from Gemini, and throughout life you'll find that this sign holds the answers to many of the dilemmas and problems which you as a Sagittarian will experience. Sagittarius and Gemini are but two sides of the same coin, and together they make a formidable team. So, find out more by turning to your opposite sign and taking a leaf out of Gemini's book.

Your love nature

Like all the Fire signs, you love the chase and can go all out to get a relationship going. You flirt, you tell jokes and you turn on all that warmth and charm. The trouble is, you can easily get bored, so you need a partner who is mentally and physically switched on, as well as one who can give you a sense of freedom. You hate being pushed into an emotional corner and tied down when you aren't ready for commitment. Nevertheless, you are romantic, loving and passionate towards your partner and a delightful friend and companion to be with.

Cosmic combinations

Whom do you get on with best? Who sets your heart on fire, puts a smile on your lips colour in your cheeks? Who brings you bliss and who gives you misery? Do you drive each other wild or up the wall? Check your love chart to find out.

Aries	passionate love	❤❤❤❤❤
Taurus	little understanding	❤
Gemini	attraction of opposites	❤❤❤❤
Cancer	occasional fling	❤❤
Leo	love fever!	❤❤❤❤❤
Virgo	picky, picky, picky	❤
Libra	sweet	❤❤❤❤
Scorpio	charmer – watch out!	❤❤
Sagittarius	wild fire	❤❤❤❤❤
Capricorn	no way	❤
Aquarius	madcap fun	❤❤❤❤
Pisces	confusing	❤❤❤

❤ = no-no

❤❤ = so-so

❤❤❤ = hang in there

❤❤❤❤ = cool couple

❤❤❤❤❤ = star match!

Talents and interests

You're an enthusiastic sports person with a love of speed and taking the odd risk or three. The desire for exploration and adventure, coupled with your talent for travel and foreign languages, can take you long distances away from home. You have an instinctive rapport with animals, especially horses of course, and this understanding gives you a keen interest in the welfare of animals in general. You're a bit of a gambler in many ways, often lucky and, fortunately for you, usually landing on your feet.

Study, work and career paths

Focus is the key word for you when it comes to studying. You're

fantastic at seeing the bigger picture, but in staring out at the middle distance you do tend to miss the detail. And when it comes to getting good marks for essays and exams, the details do matter. So don't let your eye glaze over when you're confronted with having to learn dates and figures. Find a way to commit these facts to memory and drop them into your answers where appropriate. You'll soon see your grades going up the register. One more thing – never be afraid to have a guess. You are hugely intuitive and know a lot more than you think you do. So don't leave a blank. Chances are, your guesses will hit the bull's-eye!

Your natural restlessness means that it's the more unconventional type of job that would suit you best – one which doesn't chain you to a desk or to routine hours. In fact, strict routine is a killer for you, deadening your imagination and curtailing your freedom-loving nature. Any kind of sport, of course, will draw you, whether you pursue it professionally or as an amateur. The publishing industry also appeals. You could write or edit books, sell them or work in a library. And if you could write travel features, so much the better since you'd be combining this with your other passion – globe-trotting. Teaching, translating and interpreting are equally up your street. But so too are the legal profession, veterinary work and show-biz, for you're the clown of the zodiac and adore entertaining all and sundry.

Health and beauty

Keeping active, both mentally and physically, is essential if you want to stay fit. Being out in the fresh air is good medicine for you, so walking, jogging and camping are ideal pastimes for

you to enjoy. Sagittarius rules the thighs, hips and liver, and there's a tendency to put on excess weight – not surprising since you have a huge appetite. Classically, as they get older, Sagittarians tend to put on weight around the buttocks and rump, giving them a distinctive 'pear shape'.

Female Sagittarians often have a strong, flexible and graceful body with an open, good-looking, smiley face. The males are usually tall with strong legs and thighs. They have mischievous, expressive eyes in a handsome face. Whether you're male or female, you like to dress informally, feeling most comfortable in clothes that don't restrict your movement. Beauty products that are natural and remind you of the fragrances of field flowers and woodlands are preferred.

Sign Associations

Birthstones: amethyst, turquoise

Flowers: dandelion, lilac

Colours: purple, dark blue

Trees: oak, elm

Bird: peacock

Animals: horse, stag

Foods: exotic or spicy dishes

Countries: Spain, Hungary, Australia

Body parts: liver, thighs, hips

Capricorn ♑
The Goat

22 December – 20 January
Ruling planet: Saturn
Element: Earth

Why you're lucky to be you!

If anybody's going to become rich and successful in life, it's you! You have a brilliant talent for organisation and a wonderful eye for sorting the wheat from the chaff. With masses of common sense at your disposal, you're always able to come up with practical solutions that can turn a project or situation around from something useless into a work of art. You're a realist and truly grounded, yet your sense of humour is quirky and dry, bringing flashes of fun into even the most serious of events.

You're a star because:

You're not afraid of taking the sort of tough decisions that others shy away from. You understand the meaning of duty and however old you are and whatever your size, you are prepared to carry massive responsibilities on your shoulders.

Sometimes the burdens can be overwhelming – and indeed would flatten lesser mortals – but stoically you just take it all in your stride. You're also amazingly self-disciplined and able to focus, and once you've set your mind on a particular goal you are determined to succeed, no matter how long it takes. What's more, with your in-built and infallible instinct to sniff out the best opportunities, you're bound for the top – the very, very top – of whatever ladder you choose to climb.

Your special qualities

Being a Capricorn makes you a loyal friend, capable of giving true, deep and genuine affection to those you hold dear. You're a fantastic support, ready to help, teach, share with and even prop up those in need. People know you're trustworthy and that they can rely on you. If you're given a task to do, you carry it through conscientiously and without needing any further prompting. You're blessed with an extraordinary memory and the patience to unravel the trickiest situations or the most complex of problems. Discretion is one of your best assets and you can be depended upon to keep secrets and to guard information of the greatest importance.

However...

Your ambitious drive can turn you into a bit of a workaholic. Striving to succeed or desperation to come top can lead to bitter disappointment if you don't make the grade or get the position you had set your heart on. And because money and status are so important to you, you're prone to envy those who are wealthier or better off than yourself. You're a worrier, too, and can get very stressed and pessimistic if things don't turn out the way you'd planned. Focusing on your work so much

can also make you somewhat narrow-minded so that you fail to see the value of other things around you, such as love, the beauty of Nature, and the need to laugh and sing and have fun in life.

The balancing act

Is it possible for a Capricorn like you to loosen up, pause and lift your head long enough to look out of the window and gaze at the daisies, or to take a break and smell the roses? Yet, that's the best medicine for you and all your tribe of mountain goats. Getting out into the park or garden and immersing yourself in Nature is the best way to rebalance your system and recharge your batteries. All the Earth signs tend to be introverts – although they pretend they aren't – and can become quite morose. You, especially, can get bogged down, what with your ambitions and your tendency to take on other people's problems. You must learn to recognise when enough's enough, then shut the door on your responsibilities, unwind and go out and have some fun.

The mirror effect

There's a hidden factor which many people overlook when they read about their sun sign – the *mirror effect*. Essentially, this is all about understanding your opposite sign. You see, your opposite sign is your shadow self – your other half. It complements and provides the missing links to your own character

and nature. Your opposite sign is Cancer. Understanding and adopting some of the characteristics associated with people born under this sign will help you not only to become a much more rounded person, but also to attract more good fortune into your own life. For example, Cancer can show you how to:

- make better use of your instinct, intuition and imagination

- relax and go more 'with the flow'

- appreciate the important role that relationships play in your life and wellbeing

But there's so much more that you can learn from Cancer, and throughout life you'll find that this sign holds the answers to many of the dilemmas and problems which you as a Capricorn will experience. Capricorn and Cancer are but two sides of the same coin, and together they make a formidable team. So, find out more by turning to your opposite sign and taking a leaf out of Cancer's book.

Your love nature

Though deep down inside you're a warm-hearted person, you appear rather cool and cautious when it comes to romance. The point is that you have to feel comfortable with people and get to know them before you can even start thinking about giving them your affection. Not for you the casual encounter or the one-night stand. You're far too cautious for that. You have to let love grow, and when it has and you can really trust another, that's when your earthy, passionate nature comes to the surface. And that's also when you can feel confident enough to let your sensual side come through. As a partner,

you cherish commitment and are very loyal and devoted to the one you love.

Cosmic combinations

Whom do you get on with best? Who sets your heart on fire, puts a smile on your lips and colour in your cheeks? Who brings you bliss and who gives you misery? Do you drive each other wild or up the wall? Check your love chart to find out.

Aries	immature	♥♥♥
Taurus	loving depth	♥♥♥♥♥
Gemini	flighty	♥
Cancer	attraction of opposites	♥♥♥♥
Leo	fascinating	♥♥♥
Virgo	comfortable togetherness	♥♥♥♥♥
Libra	unlikely	♥
Scorpio	mysterious fun	♥♥♥♥
Sagittarius	disconcerting	♥
Capricorn	successful duo	♥♥♥♥♥
Aquarius	inspiring	♥♥♥
Pisces	film-script romance	♥♥♥

♥ = no-no	♥♥♥♥ = cool couple
♥♥ = so-so	♥♥♥♥♥ = star match!
♥♥♥ = hang in there	

Talents and interests

You have a particular talent for getting hold of facts and building on them. You love research, whether for school or college projects or for your own interests. Because you're a traditionalist at heart, you feel a strong link with the past and with the

way things used to be done. You're fascinated, for example, by how such huge edifices as Stonehenge or the pyramids were constructed, or how past civilisations set up their constitutions and laws. But where your genius lies is in taking old technology, marrying it to the new and coming up with a pioneering masterpiece. As an Earth sign, you're in tune with the natural environment and the weather and respect the structure of ecosystems in nature. You have an aptitude for saving money by making do and mending, or by recycling or making something out of nothing.

Study, work and career paths

Studying? No problem. Hard work? Easy. Good marks? Usually. Since yours is the most industrious sign in the zodiac and you're driven by a need to succeed, you apply yourself assiduously to your work and don't rest until you get top marks. Because you're disciplined, you put homework and revision at the top of your agenda and only when it's all complete do you allow yourself time out. You can be a bit of a swot, and there's little doubt that you'll do well in your studies, but you should also allow yourself some time to have fun. You're only young once, so now and again close those books, let your hair down and go out and party.

Life for you is a serious business so you're unlikely to gravitate towards any kind of job that you deem to be silly or frivolous. Structure is so fundamental to you that the sort of professions that appeal will be involved in some way with planning and adapting, with setting up important systems, getting to the root of things and generally bringing order out of chaos. Architecture, building, planning, surveying and engineering are

typically Capricorn-type occupations. So too are high finance, business administration and politics. You'd be happy working for big corporations or in the Civil Service, say. Dentistry, osteopathy, mineralogy, farming and horticulture also appeal.

Health and beauty

Capricorns tend to walk purposefully, planting their feet in a measured way. Despite this they often fall easily and have a tendency to break bones. Capricorn rules the bones, knees and teeth, so it's wise to start taking extra care of these parts of the body from an early age. Gentle work-outs, especially for the joints – stretching, swimming, walking, skipping and trampolining – can balance your system when you feel sluggish and stressed. Like other Earth signs, you've got a strong constitution and can throw off infections quickly and endure more serious complaints bravely.

Female Capricorns usually have neat but solid and well-proportioned bodies, and attractive faces with beautiful eyes. The males often have a well-developed body, and also have attractive faces with strong jaw lines and twinkling, knowing eyes. Generally speaking, Capricorns tend to be comfortable in formal clothes, often in classical styles and usually in darker more sober colours. Because status is so important you do go for good quality items, but since you're money-conscious, too, if you can buy your designer labels at cut-down prices in the sales, so much the better.

Sign Associations

Birthstones: jet, onyx

Flower: poppy

Colours: grey, black, brown, indigo

Trees: yew, cypress, holly

Bird: vulture

Animals: goat, bear, bat

Foods: meat, root vegetables

Countries: India, Afghanistan, Mexico

Body parts: bones, knees, teeth

Aquarius ≋
The Water Carrier

21 January – 19 February
Ruling planets: Uranus, Saturn
Element: Air

Why you're lucky to be you!

Of all the signs, you have the most amazing vision. Somehow, you are able to key into the future, to see how things will be shaping up ten, twenty, thirty years from now. It's this ability that makes you appear rather spacey, far-out and, more importantly, ahead of the game. So, you've always got the latest gadget or are into the newest craze way before anyone else. When people first get to know you, they might think you're a bit bizarre, or even weird, but they soon learn to respect you as a true avant-garde and a prophet of things to come.

You're a star because:

You're the most original thinker in the whole of the zodiac. You're idealistic, constantly able to come up with new ideas and have the courage to fight for a cause you believe in. Intellectually, you're the one who takes the wider global view. Able to see the bigger picture, you dislike prejudice, oppression and social injustice of

any kind. Because you're tolerant and broad-minded, very little about human behaviour fazes you and you're prepared to live and let live. Many people mistakenly believe the two wavy lines of the Aquarius symbol represent water, but what they actually indicate are *electrical impulses* passing through the ether. Thus the symbol represents the way in which your mind works at the speed of light, from one subject to another and back again before you can blink an eye.

Your special qualities

You're a friendly, social and popular individual who makes new contacts and connections wherever you go. You have a gifted mind, especially where modern technology is concerned. Working with computers comes as second nature to you and you delight in getting onto the global network and linking with like-minded people from all corners of the world. Adaptable and resourceful, you can easily fit into any environment or group gathering and debate and discuss with vigour any issue that is aired. Incredibly inventive, you're the ultimate free thinker, always asking odd questions and seeing life from a perspective that is so different from everyone else's that it's almost as if you can see around corners. You're so unusual and the coolest mate anyone could possibly wish to have.

However...

You can be so irritating with your habit of always *knowing* everything, especially when someone is trying to tell you something they've just found out about or that they think is terribly important. Do try to keep your mouth shut, be patient and listen. It's called being tactful! You are a pioneer, that's true, and being rebellious and controversial means you dislike the

status quo. But change just for the sake of change isn't always necessary, or for the better, so don't try to force your modern ideas down people's throats. Recognise, too, that there are those who find security in the tried and trusted, even if you don't. And please remember that not everyone is as open-minded or as tolerant as you are and some of your beliefs or practices may actually shock or give offence.

The balancing act

Try to appreciate how sometimes your rebellious or way-out behaviour can create waves amongst your family, friends and neighbours and try to be more sensitive to their feelings and the way they like to live their lives. Use your talents positively and creatively to improve the lot of mankind but don't expect things to happen and change overnight. Have patience and move gracefully. Don't rock the boat unnecessarily and, as they say, 'if something ain't broke, don't try to fix it'.

The mirror effect

There's a hidden factor which many people overlook when they read about their sun sign – the *mirror effect*. Essentially, this is all about understanding your opposite sign. You see, your opposite sign is your shadow self – your other half. It complements and provides the missing links to your own character and nature. Your opposite sign is Leo. Understanding and adopting some of the characteristics associated with people born under this sign will help you not only to become a much more rounded person, but also to attract more good fortune into your own life. For example, Leo can show you how to:

- find the strength to sustain yourself

- become warmer, more tactile and more generous to others
- laugh more and have a good time

But there's so much more that you can learn from Leo, and throughout life you'll find that this sign holds the answers to many of the dilemmas and problems which you as an Aquarian will experience. Aquarians and Leos are but two sides of the same coin, and together they make a formidable team. So, find out more by turning to your opposite sign and taking a leaf out of Leo's book.

Your love nature

You tend to hide your true feelings, preferring to come across as rather distant and detached. But inside that Aquarian brain of yours, there's a lot going on as you're assessing all your options and the romantic possibilities on offer. Because you're so intellectual, your way of flirting is through conversation and by impressing your admirers with clever chat-up lines. For you, friendship in a relationship is almost more important than romance. You don't like any kind of emotional pressure and you can always find reasons to walk away from an attachment simply because it doesn't quite measure up to your ideals. However, when you do find the right companion, you make a very *exciting* partner because of your unpredictable nature and your zany character which never fails to intrigue and surprise.

Cosmic combinations

Whom do you get on with best? Who sets your heart on fire, puts a smile on your lips and colour in your cheeks? Who brings you bliss and who gives you misery? Do you drive each other wild or up the wall? Check your love chart to find out.

Aries	stimulating	❤❤❤
Taurus	slow going	❤
Gemini	terrific buzz!	❤❤❤❤❤
Cancer	vague understanding	❤
Leo	attraction of opposites	❤❤❤❤
Virgo	restrictive	❤❤
Libra	mutual minds and hearts	❤❤❤❤❤
Scorpio	mmm, unusual …	❤❤❤
Sagittarius	stimulating	❤❤❤❤
Capricorn	supportive	❤❤
Aquarius	so sussed	❤❤❤❤❤
Pisces	compassionate	❤❤❤

❤ = no-no ❤❤❤❤ = cool couple

❤❤ = so-so ❤❤❤❤❤ = star match!

❤❤❤ = hang in there

Talents and interests

You have a talent for the new and the unusual, and your
enquiring mind wants to find out how and why things work
the way they do. You can be a teacher's nightmare with your
endless questions, many of which can seem quite bizarre.
Often, though, you're more likely to seek out the answers on
your own, trawling through books at the library or logging onto
the internet to find the information you need. The sciences
attract you, particularly physics and cosmology, though you're
also intrigued by the unexplained and the paranormal – astrology and mind/body/spirit subjects, to say nothing of UFO or
crop-circle research.

Study, work and career paths

You're quite ingenious in so many ways and possess a rather 'advanced' way of thinking. You're very technologically minded and quite an expert on the computer. You're a wizard at surfing the net and happily spend hours browsing when looking for information for a special project or assignment.

You do some of your best work when studying with a group or in a team. They say that teaching is the best way to learn, and that really applies to you. So if you're revising for exams, try to explain the subject matter to one of your classmates who's not so sure of their facts. You'll both profit from the experience.

Aquarius is the researcher, inventor and humanitarian of the zodiac, and belonging to this sign means that you need the freedom to follow your instincts. Nevertheless, your approach to your work is usually logical and precise. Ordinary, routine

jobs bore you rigid and you'll find it difficult to settle happily into a standard 9 to 5 type of existence. Computer technology is definitely a big draw for you, but so too is scientific research, aeronautical engineering, astrophysics and space technology. Broadcasting would make a fine career for you, as would airline work, research or graphic art. On quite a different level, astrology would suit your enquiring mind, while healing and working in complementary medicine would give you tremendous fulfilment and satisfaction. However, you're an inventor *par excellence*, and whatever profession you follow, you'll always be thinking of new ideas to improve the work you do.

Health and beauty

Your sign rules the ankles, and many Aquarians tend to suffer with sprains to this area. Blood circulation also comes under the rulership of this sign, and to keep yours in tip-top condition you need to get plenty of fresh air and a reasonable amount of exercise. Physical activity is essential to balance and offset all the thinking and mind bending that you do. T'ai chi and chi gong are especially suitable.

Female Aquarians are usually well proportioned in the body and face. Indeed, many Aquarians are truly lovely with deep, attractive eyes which are lively when attentive and soulful when in thought. Male Aquarians tend to be fairly tall with a strong frame and a rhythmic way of moving. Their faces are handsome with eyes that penetrate and sparkle while listening to others but which seem to switch off when deep in thought. You like unusual, often ethnic, fashions and use aromatherapy and herbal products. Electric blue is a favourite colour choice in clothes.

Lucky Stars

Sign Associations

Birthstones: amethyst, blue sapphire

Flowers: snowdrop, violet

Colours: blue-green, silvery-purple

Trees: rowan, beech

Bird: peacock

Animals: whale, polar bear

Foods: grape, pomegranate

Countries: Sweden, Russia, Canada

Body parts: ankles, calves, circulatory system

Lucky Stars

Pisces ♓
The Fishes

20 February – 20 March
Ruling planets: Neptune, Jupiter
Element: Water

Why you're lucky to be you!

Of all the signs, you know what it means to experience pure joy. Holding a simple flower in your hand brings you intense pleasure; gazing at the midnight sky studded with diamond-bright stars fills you with the deepest awe and wonder; sinking your toes into the sand as you walk along the seashore transports you to heaven. For other people, these experiences are usually commonplace. For you, however, they take on a whole new meaning that heightens your senses and transforms your world into a magical wonderland. You, it seems, are in tune with the greater picture. In short, you have a direct line to the very wisdom of the universe.

You're a star because:

You're gentle and tender, sensitive, loving and very caring. You're the best friend anyone could possibly ever want: understanding, sympathetic, non-judgemental. How easy you find it

to identify with other people's feelings and how brilliant you are at listening to their problems. One of life's natural healers, you counsel silently and somehow everyone feels better just because you're there. No one can match your intuition and your psychic powers are the best. But your sense of humour is great, too, often bubbling up spontaneously like a surprise water fountain just when it's needed most.

Your special qualities

You're generous in so many ways. You give your friends not only your help and your time, but you also give away money or buy them magical gifts that you can often ill afford. Compassionate and warm-hearted, you'll stick up for anyone who's being got at or who's lonely or out of his or her depth. You just have such incredible sensitivity that you can understand what others are going through. But you also have rhythm. And how! You're musically gifted and can sing, dance and play musical instruments with tender feeling. You're artistically talented, too – brilliant at painting pictures or writing stories.

However...

Your sensitivity can go over the top sometimes and when the going gets tough you run away or fall asleep rather than confront the problem. It's your way of dealing with pressure. You can be vague and a bit of a dreamer, tending to live life with your head in the clouds – something which can annoy and exasperate the more practical people around you. Your habit of putting off until tomorrow what you could and should do today means you're in danger of missing out on golden opportunities. And you're hopeless with money. Just like the symbol

of your sign – which consists of two fishes swimming in opposite directions – you have to be careful that your cash doesn't
flow into one hand and immediately out of the other. You can
be awfully manipulative when you want to be and when things
don't go your way you tend either to overreact or to play the
martyr.

The balancing act

Discover what you're really good at and what gives you the
greatest joy in life. This is what will help you build self-confidence and good self-esteem. You're hugely creative so express
your talent for writing, painting, playing music or dancing –
whatever it is you're best at. Herein lies your clue to becoming
positive and staying cheerful and optimistic. Developing your
spiritual life, too, is important for your wellbeing. There are
many ways you can do this – for example by practising yoga,
through meditation, the martial arts, t'ai chi or chi gong. All of
these disciplines will give you just that – discipline. That's what
you need to connect with the practical, to develop your imagination and intuition while at the same time keeping your feet
on the ground.

The mirror effect

There's a hidden factor which many people overlook when
they read about their sun sign – the *mirror effect*. Essentially,
this is all about understanding your opposite sign. You see,
your opposite sign is your shadow self – your other half. It
complements and provides the missing links to your own character and nature. Your opposite sign is Virgo. Understanding
and adopting some of the characteristics associated with people
born under this sign will help you not only to become a much

more rounded person, but also to attract more good fortune into your own life. For example, Virgo can show you how to:

- cope with the everyday realities of life
- sort out your money and learn to save
- put down roots and appreciate loving stability

But there's so much more that you can learn from Virgo, and throughout life you'll find that this sign holds the answers to many of the dilemmas and problems which you as a Pisces will experience. Pisces and Virgo are but two sides of the same coin, and together they make a formidable team. So, find out more by turning to your opposite sign and taking a leaf out of Virgo's book.

Your love nature

You are the ultimate romantic! But you're a tad idealistic and your vision of relationships can be rather fairytale-ish – all roses round the door and happy-ever-afters. All Pisceans tend to look for a knight in shining armour or a princess with golden hair in a flowing gown. But having their dreams shattered, or being disappointed in love, can hurt them so deeply that they actually become ill. When you find the right soul mate, however, you're the most tender and loyal partner imaginable, able to keep the magic alive between you with your love and devotion and with the special surprises you have such a wonderful knack of conjuring up out of thin air.

Cosmic combinations

Whom do you get on with best? Who sets your heart on fire, puts a smile on your lips and colour in your cheeks?

Who brings you bliss and who gives you misery? Do you drive each other wild or up the wall? Check your love chart to find out.

Aries	exciting but exhausting	♥♥
Taurus	caring security	♥♥♥
Gemini	lacks feeling	♥♥
Cancer	love flows and flows	♥♥♥♥♥
Leo	temporary sparkler	♥♥
Virgo	attraction of opposites	♥♥♥♥
Libra	sweet diversion	♥♥♥
Scorpio	madly, deeply	♥♥♥♥♥
Sagittarius	game for a laugh	♥♥
Capricorn	supportive	♥♥♥♥
Aquarius	lukewarm	♥♥♥
Pisces	deep soul romance	♥♥♥♥

♥ = no-no	♥♥♥♥ = cool couple
♥♥ = so-so	♥♥♥♥♥ = star match!
♥♥♥ = hang in there	

Talents and interests

Your terrific eye for colour, shape and style means that you excel in creative subjects such as art and design. Your ruling planet Neptune bonds you to the sea, so you're drawn to water and to water sports. Sailing, diving, swimming or simply messing about on the beach should be high on your list of favourite activities. Like all water signs, you have great rhythm and love music. Dance, sing, start up a band – you could become famous! But Neptune also brings out other talents in you, such

as healing, for example, or a flair for acting and photography. And, don't forget, you're immensely psychic.

Study, work and career paths

You really must stop staring out of the window or going off into one of your little reveries whenever the subject matter gets too difficult. If you don't understand, ask the teacher to explain – and keep asking until the penny drops. If you don't, there'll be great gaps in your education, especially in maths and science. But you're brilliant at art, music and literature and you can write fabulous essays. You're fantastic at fiction, but remembering facts can be a problem. A good trick for you when revising is to hang up an orange-coloured poster, or to paint a wall of your bedroom orange. Psychologists say this colour helps the memory to retain information. Try it; it could make all the difference to your grades.

Because you're such a sensitive creature, you above everyone else must find the right outlet for expressing your talents, otherwise you can become very unhappy, feel sorry for yourself and just drop out. As well as the arts, the beauty and fashion industries are a natural draw. The medical profession is just up your street, too, and there's lots to choose from here, in complementary therapies as well as in conventional medicine. The theatre and the cinema call to you with your acting and musical abilities. Photography and film-making would also suit, as would writing and illustrating. And don't forget that love of water. A life on the ocean waves is not such a bad idea either.

Health and beauty

Your sign rules the feet! It means that this part of your anatomy needs particular care. That's because your feet are prone to swelling and infections. However, they will benefit from regular massage with oils; in fact, an occasional all-over body massage and a soak in a bath with glorious aromatherapy oils will do you a world of good.

Try to walk barefoot as often as you can around the house. Walk over different textures and ask for one of those wooden-beaded foot massagers for your birthday and use it every day. Throughout your life you need to be surrounded by an atmosphere of peace and calm, because negative surroundings and situations can upset your health.

In general, female Pisceans tend to be slim, but because their bodies seem to be particularly prone to holding excess water they may find their weight goes up and down. Soft greeny-grey 'liquid' eyes, tender and attractive, usually grace a pretty elfin face, which is often oval in shape. All in all, there's a touch of the 'faery queen' about them, or perhaps could it be more the look of an *angel*? Piscean males tend to be of average

height rather than tall, and have strong shoulders and a rolling, rhythmic walk. They have attractive faces with rather distinctive eyes – luminous at times but always in 'horizon search' mode.

Sign Associations

Birthstones: coral, moonstone, amethyst

Flowers: iris, water lily

Colours: blue-green, violet

Trees: willow, oak

Bird: albatross

Animals: dolphin, elephant

Foods: fruits, cucumber, seafood

Countries: Portugal, northern Spain

Body parts: feet, muscles and bones

Rising Signs

What is your rising sign?

Have you ever been to a party and someone says you look like a Scorpio and you say, well no, actually, I'm a Leo? Or do you ever read your horoscope in a magazine and think it's rubbish because what it says hardly ever comes true for you (but, okay, it's fun anyway)?

Well, the answer to all this lies in your *rising sign*.

Your astrological or zodiac sign is the one in which the sun was situated at the time you were born. The sun spends around thirty days in each sign, so if you're born in the first three weeks of June, you're going to be a Gemini. Coming into the world at Christmas time, however, makes you a Capricorn. This sign, for obvious reasons, is also called your sun sign.

But your rising sign is quite different. While your sun sign depends on the *date* of your birth, your rising sign depends on the *hour* when you're born. That's why, when an astrologer draws up your personal astrological chart, he or she needs your *precise* time of birth.

Your rising sign, which is also known as your 'ascendant', is the sign that is rising over the eastern horizon at the moment of your birth. There are twelve rising signs, just as there are twelve sun signs, and they follow each other in the same order, from Aries to Pisces. Each rising sign stays on the horizon for two hours before moving on and being replaced by the next sign in line. It all works a bit like a giant clock-face. So, your sun sign may be Taurus, for example, but if you were born in the morning your rising sign could be Cancer, let's say, although if you were born later that evening, you could be Sagittarius rising.

So why is it so important to know what your ascendant or rising sign is? Well, for a start, because it's the characteristics of this sign that describe what you look like, how you come across to the outside world and how others perceive you. So the person at that party who thinks you're a Scorpio may be right in a way, because that could well be your rising sign and that's what you're projecting – and what that person is picking up on. In many ways, your rising sign is your persona, or *mask*, and it superimposes itself on your sun sign, which is the sign that describes the person you know as your inner self.

Another reason why it's important to understand your rising sign is because it will enable you to judge more clearly the events that happen to you. Next time you read your horoscope in the paper, try reading your rising sign instead of your sun sign. You might find the predictions far more accurate.

So which is your rising sign? Well, it's a bit more difficult to calculate than your sun sign, and to be absolutely sure which of the twelve signs was on the horizon when you were born, you

need to have your birth data (the place, date and exact time of birth) calculated by a professional astrologer. However, the chart opposite provides a rough guide. It's not 100 per cent accurate because of the fast change-over of the signs, but it can be pretty close.

Find your sun sign across the top line and then run your finger down the column to the row nearest your time of birth. The symbol in the box will reveal your rising sign.

Now that you've found your rising sign, read on to reveal what it says about your image and outward appearance, how people see you and how this sign combines with your sun sign to make you the unique person that you are.

Aries rising

With Aries rising, you're likely to have a strong physique with good shoulders and strong arms and legs. Your face is lively with a lovely smile and eyes that make quick, honest and intense contact with everyone you meet. Your body movements are energetic but also graceful. Your hair, which has characteristic reddish highlights, may be thin and difficult to manage.

Other people find you open and straightforward. They especially like your humour and the fact that you're so cheerful and optimistic. You do have a tendency to push yourself forward, though, and get to the front of the queue, which can be annoying. However, you're essentially an affable type of person with a 'hail fellow well met' sort of disposition. You like people who can keep up with you, who are quick thinkers and adventurous

your sun sign	Aries ♈	Tau ♉	Gem ♊	Can ♋	Leo ♌	Vir ♍	Lib ♎	Scor ♏	Sag ♐	Cap ♑	Aqu ♒	Pisc ♓
your time of birth												
12 midnight–1am	♒	♓	♈	♉	♊	♋	♌	♍	♎	♏	♐	♑
2–4am	♓	♈	♉	♊	♋	♌	♍	♎	♏	♐	♑	♒
4–5am	♈	♉	♊	♋	♌	♍	♎	♏	♐	♑	♒	♓
6–7am	♉	♊	♋	♌	♍	♎	♏	♐	♑	♒	♓	♈
8–9am	♊	♋	♌	♍	♎	♏	♐	♑	♒	♓	♈	♉
10am–12 noon	♋	♌	♍	♎	♏	♐	♑	♒	♓	♈	♉	♊
12 noon–2pm	♌	♍	♎	♏	♐	♑	♒	♓	♈	♉	♊	♋
2–4pm	♍	♎	♏	♐	♑	♒	♓	♈	♉	♊	♋	♌
4–6pm	♎	♏	♐	♑	♒	♓	♈	♉	♊	♋	♌	♍
6–8pm	♏	♐	♑	♒	♓	♈	♉	♊	♋	♌	♍	♎
8–10pm	♐	♑	♒	♓	♈	♉	♊	♋	♌	♍	♎	♏
10–12 midnight	♑	♒	♓	♈	♉	♊	♋	♌	♍	♎	♏	♐

like yourself. But, alas, slow or weaker people tend either to annoy you or bore you rigid.

So how does your rising sign combine with your sun sign? Check it out here.

With sun in:

Aries	watch out, you can be a control freak!
Taurus	resourceful and able to carry through your plans
Gemini	highly persuasive, you can sell yourself and your ideas well
Cancer	strong family values are your springboard to success
Leo	in total and supreme command!
Virgo	highly organised and destined to succeed
Libra	strongest when working as one of a pair or in a team
Scorpio	powerfully persistent and able to re-invent yourself whenever necessary
Sagittarius	dramatic, intuitive qualities bring out your talent for leadership
Capricorn	ambitious and go-getting
Aquarius	best in group activities
Pisces	able to fulfil your potential

Taurus rising

Two types of physique are associated with Taurus rising. The first is strong, solid and earthy-looking, with an attractive, comely face. The second has a much finer bone structure and is often described as beautiful. Whichever type you are, your skin is clear and you're likely to have gorgeous eyes and attractive dimples in your cheeks. Your hands and feet are small to average, but never big. The voice is a particular asset for those born under this rising sign and it imparts a commanding presence.

With Taurus as your ascendant, your manner is bound to be pleasant but also slightly reserved. You have an outgoing, friendly smile and like to make people comfortable and feel at ease. Generally, others would describe you as charming. You always move at your own pace – unhurried but purposeful. When you're under pressure or when you want to get your point across, you can be firm – sometimes obstinate. And when you put your foot down, there's very little that will shift you.

So how does your rising sign combine with your sun sign? Check it out here.

With sun in:

Aries	very supportive nature
Taurus	determined to achieve
Gemini	motivated and constructive
Cancer	sensitive but solid
Leo	hold traditional views, values and beliefs
Virgo	competitive but thorough
Libra	artistic and practical talents combined

Scorpio	powerful personality who can make things happen
Sagittarius	your vision and good sense make you a self-improver
Capricorn	hard working and achievement motivated – you're heading for the top!
Aquarius	you'll advance through life by pooling your skills and talents with others
Pisces	good organiser who takes other people into consideration

Gemini rising

Those with Gemini rising are often fine-boned, of average size and fairly thin. The eyes are a key giveaway – they're always moving and looking around. Your hair is probably the bane of your life since it tends to be unruly and needs good cutting to keep it under control. Your feet and hands are neat and small and, like your eyes, are constantly on the move, making you the biggest fidget in the zodiac. You'll always look much younger than your age (which annoys you in your youth, but pleases you mightily as an adult).

You're a friendly dynamo, inquisitive and sometimes downright nosy. You ask direct questions and can talk to anyone about anything. You know precisely how to put on the charm when you meet new people, or want information from them. Clever and inventive, you're good at 'thinking on your feet', which can get you out of some pretty tight corners. When it comes to making up plausible excuses – you're the best in the business!

Lucky Stars

So how does your rising sign combine with your sun sign?
Check it out here.

With sun in;

Aries	need a constant stream of new people and new ideas
Taurus	honesty is the best policy if you want to win
Gemini	busy, busy, busy – do you ever stop?
Cancer	wonderfully adaptable and empathetic
Leo	very creative in the way you express yourself
Virgo	brilliant ideas and the know-how to put them into practice
Libra	tops in art and literature
Scorpio	your curious mind will discover many things
Sagittarius	lucky in personal and public relations
Capricorn	your careful planning and communication skills will make you rich
Aquarius	travel will fascinate and stimulate your mind
Pisces	networking – that's your route to fame

Cancer rising

The clues that instantly pinpoint Cancer rising are a very pale
complexion and a round, moon-shaped face, which isn't surprising since the moon is the ruler of this sign. If you're Cancer
rising you're likely to have good arms with strong shoulders
that support an impressive head, usually held high. Your eyes
are either round (again like the moon) or cat-like. Whichever,

they fix other people with a relentless stare. You're also prone to giving lots of sidelong glances that can sometimes appear furtive, even if you don't mean them to be.

People see you as pleasant and friendly, though children with Cancer rising can be a tad shy. You can be very helpful and caring to others and you're a good listener with loads of tact and discretion, though sometimes you ask some pretty direct questions. You're sympathetic – possibly too sympathetic for your own good – and worry a lot about your friends and family and take on their problems as if they were your own. You don't like confrontation and become withdrawn and moody if upset – and then you quietly and deliberately plot your revenge!

So how does your rising sign combine with your sun sign? Check it out here.

With sun in:

Aries	impulsive and energetic
Taurus	attract good fortune
Gemini	keeper of secrets and secret documents
Cancer	deeply caring and tender
Leo	bright star in the family
Virgo	great at practical planning
Libra	thrive on family happiness
Scorpio	feel things deeply
Sagittarius	generous and with inspired ideas
Capricorn	reserved and cautious

Aquarius	psychic
Pisces	intuitively gifted

Leo rising

Think of the proud lion and his slow, purposeful movements and you get a description of Leo rising. Having Leo as your ascendant suggests you have a good head of hair. It's your crowning glory because, after all, it's your mane! Your profile and attractive eyes are lion- or cat-like, and you have high cheekbones. You walk tall, holding your head up high in a regal manner, and you move with a graceful dignity.

Mostly, your friendly manner and ability to listen and talk to others inspires confidence. Sometimes, though, you can come across as arrogant, thinking your ideas are better than anyone else's. You like to be popular, adore being centre-stage and made a fuss of. Luckily for you, you are generally well liked, because basically you're fun to be with. You also have a knack of attracting good fortune – perhaps because, again like a cat, you always land on your feet.

So how does your rising sign combine with your sun sign? Check it out here.

With sun in:

Aries	idealistic crusader
Taurus	deeply indulgent
Gemini	able to promote yourself intelligently
Cancer	need plenty of praise

Leo	what pizzazz!
Virgo	selective, very selective
Libra	expensive tastes
Scorpio	steamy passion flower
Sagittarius	stage-struck
Capricorn	seriously upwardly mobile
Aquarius	philanthropic
Pisces	potential to become a great actor

Virgo rising

This rising sign suggests a tall body with neat, strong bone structure. With this ascendant, you probably have a pale skin, are good looking, and when you smile your eyes suddenly light up and radiate a natural charm. Your hand movements are very deft, but you can be clumsy if you lose concentration. Your posture is good, though you can seem overly tense. Noted for your tidy mind, you usually appear neat and trim.

Your sense of humour is quick and quirky, with an ability to see the bizarre in everyday situations. You come across as essentially clever, confident and polite, although you can appear cool and slightly withdrawn when meeting new people. Others see you as being very 'together' and unflappable, because, whatever crisis occurs, you always seem to have presence of mind. However, when you're really anxious, nervous or upset, you get stomach ache, which is absolutely typical of this rising sign.

So how does your rising sign combine with your sun sign? Check it out here.

With sun in:

Aries	brilliant innovator
Taurus	practical, hard-working and doggedly persistent
Gemini	highly skilled with your hands
Cancer	your friends are like family
Leo	strength of will overcomes all difficulties
Virgo	organised and efficient
Libra	brains and beauty combined
Scorpio	X-ray vision
Sagittarius	disciplined brilliance
Capricorn	industrious
Aquarius	original and inventive mentality
Pisces	able to make dreams come true

Libra rising

Libra rising is often the sign of a real beauty or a handsome man, with good skin, and often with fair hair and lovely eyes. If Libra was ascending at the moment of your birth, you're likely to have attractive, well-balanced and refined features. Physically well built, chances are you'll be of average height and have both graceful posture and fluid movement as you walk. You like to appear well dressed, preferring quality gear and designer labels, because for you, image is everything.

People are immediately struck by your quiet, sensitive and friendly manner and find you easy to get along with. You have a terrific, natural charm so it's no effort to talk and listen to others when you're in company. You're intelligent and engaging with an enquiring nature. However, you need to watch for those moments when you are just plain lazy and can't summon up a single ounce of enthusiasm to do anything. Justice is important to you so you insist on fairness, but your charm can sometimes become oleaginous – which means just a tad smarmy.

So how does your rising sign combine with your sun sign? Check it out here.

With sun in:

Aries	powerful motivator
Taurus	big spender
Gemini	terrific writer
Cancer	great counsellor and judge
Leo	able to attract powerful and influential friends
Virgo	special talent for detailed planning
Libra	very laid back
Scorpio	can spot quality a mile off
Sagittarius	wisdom of Solomon
Capricorn	an eye for only the best
Aquarius	unique creative expression
Pisces	painstakingly sympathetic

Scorpio rising

There's something different, even mysterious, about people who are born when Scorpio is rising. It's all in the eyes. If this is your ascendant, you're likely to have an almost hypnotic gaze which people find compelling. Your voice, too, is impressive and altogether there is a magnetic quality about you that is quite irresistible. Probably well built with strong shoulders, long arms and smallish hands and feet, you move with good rhythm and with a certain 'presence' which makes you stand out in a crowd.

You come across as a powerful personality, commanding respect. But you can attract jealousy, too, which you immediately detect because you posses a very strong sixth sense. It takes a lot to make you angry but when you are, you erupt like a volcano. You don't suffer fools gladly and you can floor an opponent with just one of your fierce looks. Most of the time, however, your manner is charming and laid back, and when you're relaxed you've got a crazy sense of humour which you use in a clever, satirical way. This makes you popular with people of all ages.

So how does your rising sign combine with your sun sign? Check it out here.

With sun in:

Aries	love a challenge
Taurus	able to attract wealth
Gemini	brilliant at maths and calculation
Cancer	psychically gifted

Leo	potential for fame
Virgo	supreme powers of concentration
Libra	secretive
Scorpio	hidden depths
Sagittarius	financially lucky
Capricorn	able to keep secrets
Aquarius	attract and keep unusual friends
Pisces	musically accomplished

Sagittarius Rising

Those with Sagittarius rising are described as handsome people with firm jaw lines and expressive eyes. If you're one of these, you'll know what a relaxed, sporty kind of person you are, preferring to wear comfortable gear rather than smart clothes that cramp your style. However, when you do have to dress up, you scrub up spectacularly well! Usually athletic in stature, your hair is thick and abundant (though men are particularly prone to balding when older).

As a rule, you come across as a friendly, affable individual, pleasant, non-confrontational and thoroughly honest. You're inquisitive and find it easy to approach people and engage them in conversation. It's your enthusiasm, infectious laughter and disarmingly open smile that everyone responds to. So much so, in fact, that you'll find throughout your life even total strangers are so comfortable in your presence they will pour out their life history to you – whether you want to hear it not.

So how does your rising sign combine with your sun sign? Check it out here.

With sun in:

Aries	your originality will score in the worlds of sport and ideas
Taurus	you'll always know how to make money
Gemini	a special genius for public relations
Cancer	cast-iron instincts will make you a fortune
Leo	able to achieve global respect, fame and success
Virgo	can see the whole picture
Libra	your contacts will all be influential ones
Scorpio	a rich imagination is your route to success
Sagittarius	optimistic, fun-loving wanderer
Capricorn	following your hunches will make you a winner
Aquarius	full of ingenious ideas
Pisces	a natural philosopher, teacher or healer

Capricorn rising

This rising sign endows people with good bone structure. In fact, those born in this group are often considered 'bony'. Many have prominent knees. Having this ascendant gives you an attractive face, large eyes and a cautious smile. Your hair is likely to have a mind of its own and need regular cutting to keep it under control. You walk in a purposeful manner with a slight forward lean. You can be light on your feet but some-

times you have difficulty with your balance and trip over, which can lead to broken bones. Practical and comfortable is your preferred dress style – slightly traditional but always expensive looking.

No matter how old you are, you always come across as mature, attentive and business-like. There's a strong streak of dependability about you and your calmness inspires confidence. Ambitious, thorough and conscientious, you work hard. You have high standards and expect everyone else to strive as hard as you do. When others get to know you better, they find your dry sense of humour a delight, and being a good listener makes you popular, too.

So how does your rising sign combine with your sun sign? Check it out here.

With sun in:

Aries	self-motivated – you know where you're going
Taurus	hard work and creative talents will ensure a good living
Gemini	high-flyer
Cancer	solid and very grounded
Leo	only the best is good enough for you
Virgo	organised and efficient – you're a mean machine
Libra	class act
Scorpio	seriously sound

Sagittarius	great mind for planning big projects
Capricorn	disciplined and ambitious workaholic
Aquarius	ingenious ideas will take you far
Pisces	tough cookie with a soft centre

Aquarius rising

People with Aquarius rising are often considered real beauties. This ascendant gives you well-developed features, a square forehead and defined eyebrows. Your eyes twinkle with good humour and your smile is friendly and open. Your hair is probably thick and abundant and tends to do its own thing! Often of average height, you're shapely and graceful and you carry yourself with a certain nobility which can often make others look at you twice.

You're sometimes quiet and sometimes the life and soul of the party, but you're always friendly and full of original ideas. It's all part of that unpredictable side of your nature which makes you so interesting to know, especially when you do something unexpected – which you very often tend to do. You'll speak your mind when necessary and if you're challenged you're quick to reply with just the right cryptic phrase or witty remark. You like to be surrounded by friends and are brilliant at sussing out what's going on in other people's minds.

So how does your rising sign combine with your sun sign? Check it out here.

With sun in:

Aries	brilliant inventive mind
Taurus	unusual ideas give you a leading edge in creative projects
Gemini	computer and technological skills *par excellence*
Cancer	perceptive
Leo	popular leader
Virgo	medically minded
Libra	seeker of truth and harmony
Scorpio	social reformer
Sagittarius	great accomplishments
Capricorn	high ideals
Aquarius	revolutionary ideas
Pisces	genuine and generous

Pisces rising

One of the most distinctive features of Pisces rising is the colour of the eyes, which are usually greeny-grey or light blue. There's a definite aqua tint to them which befits the water element ruling this sign and gives the eyes a translucent softness. Belonging to this ascendant is likely to make you of average height with a personable appearance and fine fair hair. You're not hugely image-conscious and you like to stick to the colours and styles that 'feel right' for you.

You have a natural, open manner and when meeting new

people you come across as helpful and concerned. You deal with folk in a courteous way and like to be treated with the same respect. You don't work well under pressure and you give the impression of being a bit of a dreamer, which can make others think that you're unreliable. In fact, you're quick to read people and have the ability to assess situations at a glance.

So how does your rising sign combine with your sun sign? Check it out here.

With sun in:

Aries	quiet strength
Taurus	intuitive creator
Gemini	inspired writer
Cancer	soft, tender, emotional and sentimental
Leo	will shine with backing and support
Virgo	strong judgement
Libra	so arty but also so indecisive
Scorpio	powerfully insightful
Sagittarius	a born guru with deep wisdom
Capricorn	good psychological grasp of people
Aquarius	wonderfully caring
Pisces	a truly kind soul

Thank Your Lucky Stars!

I hope *Lucky Stars* has given you some valuable knowledge and, perhaps, a better understanding of who you are. I hope, too, that it has confirmed some of the things that you *thought* you knew about yourself but weren't 100 per cent sure about – your latent talents, your special qualities, your hopes, dreams, expectations and those characteristics that make you the wonderful person you are. If, in holding up a mirror, this book has also reflected some of your not-so-good points, don't be downhearted. Look on this as an opportunity for growth and increased wisdom, because by recognising these characteristics you can work on the negative aspects of your nature that hold you back. So, in the words of that very old song, 'you gotta accentuate the positive and eliminate the negative' to find happiness and success.

But the real message in *Lucky Stars* is that you're *special*. No matter which sign of the zodiac you belong to, *you* matter and you make a difference. You have a place in this world and an important role to play. Pursue your dream and each and every day acknowledge your blessings and truly thank your lucky stars.

Lori ☆